# CROCHET FOR BEGINNERS

Ultimate Guide with Basic Techniques, Helpful Tips and Tricks & Easy Patterns to Get Started | Be Surprised by the Calming Therapy of Crocheting, Working Away Unneeded Tension

## Hillary Wire

© **Copyright 2020 - All rights reserved**.

This document is geared towards providing exact and reliable information in regard to the topic and issue covered.

- From a Declaration of Principles which was accepted and approved equally by a Committee of the American Bar Association and a Committee of Publishers and Associations.

In no way is it legal to reproduce, duplicate, or transmit any part of this document in either electronic means or in printed format. All rights reserved.

The information provided herein is stated to be truthful and consistent, in that any liability, in terms of inattention or otherwise, by any usage or abuse of any policies, processes, or directions contained within is the solitary and utter responsibility of the recipient reader. Under no circumstances will any legal responsibility or blame be held against the publisher for any reparation, damages, or monetary loss due to the information herein, either directly or indirectly.

Respective authors own all copyrights not held by the publisher.

The information herein is offered for informational purposes solely and is universal as so. The presentation of the information is without contract or any type of guarantee assurance.

The trademarks that are used are without any consent, and the publication of the trademark is without permission or backing by the trademark owner. All trademarks and brands within this book are for clarifying purposes only and are owned by the owners themselves, not affiliated with this document.

# Table of Contents

**Introduction** ............................................................................. **7**

    What Is Crochet? ................................................................. 7

    What Are the Health Benefits of Crochet? ......................... 7

    The History of Crochet ....................................................... 8

    Getting Started and Common Crochet Terms .................. 10

**Chapter 1. The Crocheting Toolbox** ...................................... **23**

    Materials ............................................................................ 23

    A Calm, Perfect Crocheting Location ............................... 33

**Chapter 2. Simple Stitches and Techniques** ......................... **44**

    Slip Stitch ........................................................................... 44

    Slipstitch ............................................................................ 44

    Chain Stitch ....................................................................... 45

    Single Crochet Stitch ......................................................... 45

    Half-Double Crochet Stitch .............................................. 46

    Double Crochet Stitch ...................................................... 46

    Triple Crochet Stitch ........................................................ 47

    Double Triple Crochet Stitch ........................................... 48

    Overcasting ....................................................................... 48

## Chapter 3. Stitch Variations ................................................ 49

Back Loop Stitch ............................................................ 49

Front Loop Stitch ........................................................... 49

Extended Stitch ............................................................. 50

## Chapter 4. Relief Stitches and Raised Stitches .................. 51

Front Post Stitch ............................................................ 51

Back Post Stitch ............................................................. 51

Raised Rib Stitching ....................................................... 52

Basketweave Stitching .................................................... 52

Crossed Stitch ................................................................ 53

Spike Stitch ................................................................... 53

## Chapter 5. Techniques ........................................................ 55

How to Crochet for Right-Handers .................................. 55

How to Crochet for Left-handers .................................... 58

What Is the Difference Between Right and Left-Handed Crafters? ... 61

How to Hold Hook and Yarn ........................................... 62

## Chapter 6. Alternative Crochet Methods ........................... 69

Tunisian Crochet ............................................................ 69

Broomstick' Crochet ....................................................... 70

Crocheting with Pretty Beads ................................................................ 71

## Chapter 7. How to Understand Patterns ............................................ **74**

What Is a Crochet Pattern? ................................................................. 74

How to Read a Crochet Pattern .......................................................... 74

Pattern Abbreviations ......................................................................... 75

How to Decipher the Puzzle That Is a Crochet Pattern ..................... 79

Pattern Charts ..................................................................................... 83

## Chapter 8. Easy and Fun Projects ....................................................... **87**

Tote Bag .............................................................................................. 87

Beanie .................................................................................................. 90

Coasters ............................................................................................... 93

Cute Toothbrush Holder or Cup Cozy ............................................... 95

Fingerless Gloves ................................................................................ 98

Pot Holders ....................................................................................... 100

Simple, Flowy Scarf .......................................................................... 102

Washcloths ........................................................................................ 105

Broomstick Crochet Scarf ................................................................ 106

## Conclusion ........................................................................................... **108**

# Introduction

## What Is Crochet?

Crochet is a delightful art form that incorporates loops and stitches of yarn into products such as clothing, homewares, and decorations. It uses a single hook to link these loops and create rows of stitching that eventually become the finished product. The term crochet has French roots and roughly translates to 'hook.'

## What Are the Health Benefits of Crochet?

Believe it or not, crocheting is good for your health! Crocheting is a wonderful hobby once you get the hang of it, and it has been linked to lower blood pressure, improved breathing, and a better mood due to its stress-reducing qualities. It also reduces your probability of having an anxiety attack, improves anxiety in general, and can calm you down after a long, hard day.

The repetition of your crocheting movements creates a lull that has been linked to these calming qualities of the craft. Additionally, it lowers your anxiety and boosts your mood when you create something tangible, giving you a sense of pride and accomplishment. This will improve your drive, your focus, and your overall self-esteem.

Due to the boost in mood and the release of serotonin, some have linked crocheting to a decrease in depression symptoms. It has also been linked to a major improvement in insomnia due to its lulling and calming properties through the rhythm of the repetitive actions involved.

The brain function and memory practice involved with the use of crochet and as a craft it greatly improved the memory-processing sections of the brain. Remembering the loop structures, patterns, techniques, and crochet rows all work together to improve your overall brain function. Because of this, doctors have linked crochet to a reduced risk of developing Alzheimer's. Crocheting cuts the risk of this disease in half, and it is a nice way to preserve your mind for the future.

## The History of Crochet

The history of crochet is pretty short and sweet, but it is interesting, nonetheless. In the early nineteenth century, it was referred to as a form of knitting in Europe. Specifically, it was named shepherd's knitting. It was seen as inferior to knitting due to the inexpensive nature of the craft. More people were able to afford crochet supplies than knitting, particularly due to the purchase of only one hook and the fact that most fabrics and yarns could be used to produce a finished product.

Once crochet, or shepherd's knitting, grew in popularity among commoners, Queen Victoria of Great Britain caught wind of it. She discovered the charm and beauty of the craft after purchasing a lovely crocheted lace piece from a poor Irish woman. She had seen the woman struggling after the famine in Ireland, and she quickly fell in love with the lace piece. Soon after, the queen learned how to crochet herself. She made many scarves, which she gave as gifts to war veterans. The art of crochet quickly spread like wildfire after that, and most of England and Europe embraced the delightful hobby.

The origins of the word crochet come from France. The word crochet means hook, and those who participated in crochet later added the extra t. As crochet is practiced with a hook and yarn, this name is quite fitting.

After the turn of the century, crochet became popular in the modern world. Around the 1920s, people started turning away from crocheting decorations and began to use it as a way to make clothing. The cloche hat, beautifully crocheted dresses, and more were invented and loved around these times.

About twenty years later, during the Second World War, crochet became a popular way to save money on clothing. To help the war effort, women took to crocheting and added some warmth and fashion to the troops.

Then comes the 1950s! Now that the war was over, the ladies turned their attention back to crocheted fashion. They started making beautiful day dresses out of crocheted patterns, handcrafted shawls and hats, and even crocheted chic, lovely wedding dresses.

After the 1960s hit, crochet really started to pick up momentum! In fact, crochet blossomed and bloomed most in the sixties and the seventies. Crochet evolved from clothing alone to pillow covers, housewares, and even hammocks! Crocheted fashion also became more modern and comfortable, featuring flowing, warm dresses, form-fitting crocheted skirts, and more. Blankets, overalls, hats, and vests became a colorful trend for the crocheting world, and people began to get creative with new shapes and aesthetics. The crocheted square, or granny square, is a good example of this.

Even today, crochet is quite popular and calming, though many see it as a hobby rather than a large fashion trend. Regardless of the reason you crochet, however, it is not hard to see the impact that it has had on the world. You can let crochet impact your life and the lives of those around you as well if you so choose. Take the crafting world by storm and show people that crochet is here to stay!

## Getting Started and Common Crochet Terms

### Common Crocheting Terms

Here is a list of the terms we will be using throughout this book. Refer to this list if you get confused about the crocheting phrases we will be discussing going forward.

- Amigurumi – We will not be going over amigurumi patterns in this book, as it is a more advanced technique, but amigurumi is the practice of crocheting plush toys, such as stuffed animals and dolls. The term has Japanese origins, and it roughly translates to "crocheted stuffed doll."
- Appliqué – This fancy word has a simple definition. Appliqué, in respect to crochet, is the technique of sewing crocheted shapes, patterns, and motifs onto your crochet project or an item such as a towel, pillow, or other items. It is a decoration technique that gives your project flair and personality!

- Back or Front Loops – When you see a loop mentioned in a crochet pattern, it pertains to the direction in which you will insert your hook when creating a stitch. A front loop will go in through the front, and a back loop will go into the back. Some stitches, like a standard stitch, will have you doing both. When you make only a front loop, you are going to be inserting the hook into the loop that is facing you, and the back loop will be the side facing away from you.
- Block – In crochet, a block is an angular shape, such as a square, that is worked into rows and rounds that act similarly to patchwork to make intricate designs. These designs are repeated to make motifs and similar projects.
- Blocking – Blocking your crochet project means that you flatten it out by pinning it to a smooth surface and steaming it to hold it in place. When it dries, it will hold its shape.
- Chain – A chain is the basis of all crochet patterns and projects. It forms the foundation for the rows you will build upon throughout the process of creating your piece. The first chains in your patterns will be referred to as the foundation chains, in fact, and they determine how wide the piece will be. Chains can also determine the height of each row. When the chain starts the row, it is called a turning chain. You can also use your chains to make spaces or gaps in the design for a unique look. This is mostly used in designs that incorporate lace, but you can get creative with it!

- Chain Space – Put simply, the chain space is the space between each of your chain stitches.
- Chevron – Chevron is a crocheting formation that creates a zig-zag design. It is created through a variety of increases and decreases in the stitching.
- Cluster – A cluster is a group of stitches that is gathered up in one place. You can use a cluster to make pretty designs, such as a shell or a half-circle, and they can add texture to your projects. You can make a cluster as big or small as you like, and its size is determined by the number of stitches incorporated into the cluster. When you encounter a cluster in a crochet pattern, it will always tell you the number of stitches that will be in the cluster.
- Corner-to-Corner or C2C – This simply means that you crochet in a diagonal fashion, and it is very easy to do!
- Drape – The drape of your yarn or piece as a whole pertains to its ability to be flexible and hang in a certain way. The more your crochet project drapes, the better its flow will be. Lighter yarns have a more fluid drape, and bulkier yarns have a more solid, immobile drape.
- Edging – Crochet edging is the practice of making decorative stitching designs on the edges of your projects.
- Embellish – When you embellish your crochet or embellish an item with crochet accents, it means that you are adding to it and decorating it in a certain way. You can embellish your scarf pattern with beads, your decorative patterns with ribbons, or your

pillowcases with motifs. You can embellish items with crochet rounds and other stitching techniques. Embellishments add to your projects and give them a nice, decorative boost!

- Gauge – The gauge refers to the number of stitches and rows in a measurement of space in the project. It includes a recommended size for the hook you will use in a pattern as well.
- Increase and Decrease – When you see the words increase or decrease in a pattern, it is referring to the act of reducing or adding stitches. When you increase a stitch, you add more stitches into the same place on the pattern. When you decrease, you turn multiple stitches into one. It can get a little bit confusing at times, but once you make a few patterns, it will begin to make more sense!
- Intarsia – Intarsia is a fancy way of saying that you use multiple colors in your design by switching between yarns of different colors.
- Magic Loop, Magic Circle, Drawstring Loop, or Adjustable Loop – These terms all mean the same thing, and they refer to a technique that you will start your pattern with. It is used with round projects, and it lets you make the hole in your first round nearly invisible through the process of tightening the loop and the stitches in the round.
- Mesh – A mesh crochet design is where you stitch the chains farther apart to leave gaps in the pattern, which creates a grid of stitches and spaces.

- Motif – A motif is the same as a block, but it is worked in a circular shape, or crochet round, instead of an angular shape.
- Picot – Picots are loops of chains that are used for decoration, and they are normally quite small. They are predominantly used to make an effect called a trefoil, and they are very pretty!
- Post Stitches – A post stitch is a stitch in which you inject your crochet hook around the stitch instead of into the stitch. It gives a raised and ribbed texture to your projects, and it is often used with clothing, pillowcases, and blankets. Post stitches are split into two categories, which are the front and the back post. This simply defines into which direction you insert the hook.
- Relief Stitch – A relief stitch is a stitching technique in which you work over other stitches to create a design or pattern. It adds texture and visualization to your piece.
- Repeat – The repeat in a pattern pertains to a particular amount of stitches or rounds that are needed to complete a single stitch in a pattern.
- Right and Wrong Side – The right or wrong side of your project simply refers to the side of the project on which you primarily work and the opposite side. When you work a pattern, the side you are directly facing is the right side. If the pattern wants you to work on the wrong side, you just flip the project over. Another way to look at it is that the front of the original stitches is the right side, and the back of the stitches is the wrong side.

- Round – In a crochet pattern, the crochet round is a row of stitches that goes in a circular pattern to make a round project such as a coaster, doily, placemat, or similar item.
- Row – A row in a pattern is a line of stitches that you crochet and build upon one another to complete the project. For instance, a scarf could have a row of ten stitches repeated over and over until it creates the length of the scarf that you desire.
- Skein – a skein of yarn is like a ball of yarn, but it is in a different shape. Most yarn is sold in skeins with a label or ribbon securing it all together. Normally, skeins are composed of large loops of yarn and secured with the label or ribbon.
- Wave – Crocheting soft wave patterns through times increases and decreases in the pattern.
- Yarn Weight – When we talk about the weight of yarn, we are not talking about how much it weighs in pounds or ounces. The weight of a yarn pertains to its thickness or thinness, and it is how different yarn types are categorized. For instance, the bulky yarn has a higher weight than thin, lacy yarn. The yarn is categorized in weights to give you a better idea of the hook diameter you will need to use with it, as well as the overall look of the finished project.
- Yarnover – A yarnover occurs when you wrap your yarn around or over your crochet hook. It is a simple term that is used in many patterns, and you will encounter it often when doing many different types of projects.

## General Crocheting Tips and Tricks

1. Whenever you create seams on your project, use the yarn that was used in the main project to give it a more fluid look.
2. While starting out, in addition to reading books like this one, it is a good idea to watch videos and look at pictures of people crocheting so you can get a visual feel for the craft. You can also take crocheting classes, but those can cost money, so it is a matter of preference.
3. Keep your supplies organized and in a designated area, so you never lose what you need. You can have it all in one place so you can use it as needed. A set of drawers, shelves, or a crochet bag are all good options.
4. You can supplement larger, trickier projects with small, simple projects. This will break up the frustration of working with a larger piece.
5. Mark your rows with pins or a row marker in order to stay on track.
6. You can make a visual representation of complicated patterns, or any patterns, on a spreadsheet to make it easier to follow. You can even print the spreadsheet out so you can mark your rows off as you go.
7. If you accidentally buy a crochet hook that does not fit into your hand correctly or is uncomfortable, you can use modeling clay to sculpt a better handle around the hook. You can customize it to the exact measurements of your hand.

8. If you cannot fit your yarn into a tapestry needle, a simple solution is to twist the end of the yarn and paint the edge with clear, fast-drying nail polish. Once it dries, it should slip right through. After you finish sewing the yarn through your project, you can snip off the hardened edge.
9. Try not to iron your crochet pieces when trying to flatten them. Instead, pin your piece down and spray it with water. Then, it will retain its shape when it dries. You can also use a mixture of starch and water to get similar results.
10. Keep a detailed list of the hook types and yarn varieties you have, as well as the amount of yarn you have left, so you never over or under-buy supplies.
11. When you get a new skein of yarn, it is a good idea to unravel it and remake it into a ball for easier use during crocheting.
12. Ensure you keep your yarn ball in a position with which it will be easy to crochet fluidly. If you have to readjust your yarn constantly, it can add unnecessary amounts of time to your project.
13. Unless you are switching yarn types, don't change out your crochet hooks during the same project. It can make it look less cohesive and change the overall look of the piece.
14. Be creative and experiment if you think of ways to change up a project. It is ok to divert from the pattern at times.
15. Join a crocheting community or social media group to find friends who can crochet with you and share helpful information with you!

16. Start with simple patterns, then work your way up as you get comfortable with different stitching styles. Start with small patterns that use basic stitches, then slowly add more challenging patterns to keep you on your toes as you learn.
17. Practice holding your crochet hook in different ways. There is no one way to hold your hook, and we'll cover that later. Experiment with hook-holding styles to find what is best for you.
18. If you get frustrated with a project, set it aside, and come back to it at a later time to minimize stress and aggravation.
19. Keep a notepad near you while you crochet to take notes of your experience. Write down what works for you, what doesn't, and ideas that you may have for future projects.
20. Try out ergonomic hooks for a unique and fluid crochet style. They come in many shapes and sizes, and handcrafted ones have gorgeous designs! They are very easy on the hands as well.
21. Store your yarn in clear, plastic tubs to keep them out of the way while being able to see what is inside. This is a great organization technique that will keep your crochet station nice, tidy, and easy to work with.
22. If your yarn gets a bit rough, or it is purchased rough, you can soften it in a variety of ways. The most common way to do this is to wash it and fluff it to soften it. Then, you rinse it and repeat a few times to get the softness level you desire.
23. Try to crochet at least fifteen minutes a day to keep up your skills, if you like. It will give you a moment of peace and practice during

the day, and you can always expand the time depending on the projects that you have.
24. Try to focus on crocheting things that you enjoy. If you don't like what you are making, you won't be as invested in it, and it will not come out as well. Put your heart into it, and your projects will turn into masterpieces!
25. It is very important to keep track of your rows. Keep count of them, so you don't lose track and end up lengthening or shortening your project by accident.
26. If you make a mistake, do not be discouraged. Learn from it or make it your own!
27. Take pictures of your first projects, so you have something fond to look back on. It can also encourage you to do bigger and more challenging projects, and it can show you your progress along the way.
28. When in doubt, start over. If you mess up a few stitches or lose track, there is no shame in starting over.
29. Always take periodic breaks while crocheting, so you don't strain your wrist.
30. Read through a pattern a few times before you begin your project, so you know what to do beforehand. You want to familiarize yourself with the pattern, so you don't miss-steps along the way.
31. Change your grip periodically on your crochet hook, so your hand does not get tired.

32. It's a good idea to listen to calming music while you work or light some soothing candles to get you in a good mood while crocheting.
33. You can use a stress ball to prepare your hand for crocheting, and it can be calming to use when you are frustrated.
34. Make sure you sit in a comfortable place while crocheting, so your body does not get stiff or sore.
35. Store metal tapestry needles by including a magnet that will keep them all together. This will keep them from moving around, getting lost, or poking you.
36. You can store crochet hooks in a pencil holder or a small utensil bag.
37. You can substitute thicker yarns by doubling up on thinner yarn to give your project the correct size.
38. If your yarn is frayed and you need to thread a tapestry needle, you can pinch the yarn in half and pull the pinched section of the yarn through so the frayed part can slip right through.
39. You can make your own yarn bowl by taking a normal bowl and a binder clip. Clip the binder clip to the edge of the bowl and thread the yarn between the clasps to get a tangle-free yarn bowl!
40. If you do not have a stitch marker, you can also use a bobby pin, paper clip, or similar items in a pinch!
41. Save projects from unraveling by creating a loop and inserting a stitch marker.
42. Set a timer while you work so you can take breaks. While crocheting, you can get lost in your work and forget to take care of

yourself. Setting a timer reminds you to get up, stretch, drink some water, and rest your hands before you get back to work.

43. Make sure you research your supplies before you buy them. Don't simply buy cheap supplies for convenience, but you should also avoid spending too much. Expensive supplies do not necessarily equate to quality supplies, so choose what works best for you and your projects.

44. Label your projects when you store them, so you remember what you were working on. Either keep a printed copy of the pattern with the project, marked with the stopping point, or add a sticky note or similar marker. This will help you pick up where you left off with minimal confusion.

45. Make a small crochet tool kit to throw in your purse so you can crochet on the go. That way, you will have something to do when waiting for appointments or similar situations.

46. An easy way to count your stitches is to look at the little Vs. at the tops of the stitches. This is easier for your eye to follow, and you won't lose your place as often.

47. Make sure you have enough yarn for the pattern before starting the pattern. This will save you headaches down the road.

48. Always read your yarn labels to know what you are working with.

49. Always be open to learning more, no matter how experienced you get. It is always helpful to expand your knowledge.

50. Find a brand of yarn that you really like and stick with it. You can branch out to other yarns as well, but finding one that you really love is a great feeling.

# Chapter 1. The Crocheting Toolbox

## Materials

First off, we will go over crochet hooks and yarn, as those are the two most important parts of the crocheting process. Without one or the other, you don't have the means to crochet. They come in many yards, pertaining to yarn, or and many millimeters, pertaining to hooks. Then, we will go over every other material that you will need to complete your crocheting toolbox!

## Crochet Hooks

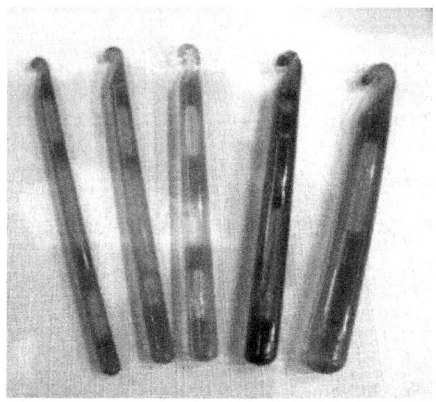

Crochet hooks come in many shapes, sizes, and colors, and they all have their own particular uses. Many crochet hook sizes are specifically made to accommodate certain yarn weights, which we will go over in a moment, and the type of hook you use can determine the ease and aesthetic of your piece. Crochet hooks can be made from a variety of materials, such as metal, bamboo, plastic, and even ivory. There are also different crochet hooks for different crochet techniques, and there are crochet hooks catered to comfort and other crocheting styles. There are comfort-grip hooks, ergonomic hooks to reduce wrist strain, double-ended hooks with two different sized hooks, Tunisian hooks, and more! Whichever way you prefer to crochet, there is a hook out there for you!

The size of a crochet hook correlates with its usefulness when used with certain yarn weights. Their diameters are measured in millimeters around the hook's shaft. The hook's diameter helps you create a certain size or aesthetic for the stitches in the project patterns. The Diameters range from around half a millimeter to over fifteen millimeters, depending on what project type and yarn weight you are going for. Most, if not all, crochet hooks will have a mark on them with which you can determine the size of the hook.

The material of these hooks gives a different feel to the crocheting process, and depending on your preference; it can make the crocheting process smoother and more enjoyable. The look of the material is one aspect of preference, as is the glide of the yarn and the ease at which you can hold the hook. Wood and bamboo hooks are popular among those with arthritis and similar health issues due to their flexibility.

Generally, steel and other metal hooks are used for smaller projects, such as lacework and lighter yarn weights. Plastic and bamboo hooks are more flexible and are used in many sizes, though they are most often used for medium to large yarn weights and most projects. Wooden hooks are generally hand-made and can be used for most types of crochet. They will likely not work with very heavy yarns like jumbo, as the wood may break, but there are some flexible woods that would do well in this regard. Make sure to take the material into account when considering how heavy of a hook you would like. If you go with lighter hook material, such as plastic, aluminum, or wood, it may cause you to have less wrist strain over time, as your wrist muscles will not need to sustain the extra weight. If you go with heavier material, such as certain metals and other materials, it may increase the strain that you will acquire in your wrist through repeated stitching and movement.

The hook has five main parts. It is a great idea to learn the names of these parts early so you will know what to do while reading a pattern. The five parts of a crochet hook are the tip, the throat, the shank, the grip, and the handle. The tip is the top-most part of the hook, and it is normally pointed. Next is the throat, which can be rounded or cut-in, depending on the type of hook you are using. Below the throat is the shank, which will hold most of your stitches. Then there is the grip, where you will primarily hold the hook and control its movement. Under this is the handle or the bottommost part of the crochet hook.

The tip of the crochet hook is the part that gets inserted into the stitches and chains of your progress in preparation for making more chains and stitches. Its sharpness allows it to penetrate the small openings between the yarn, so the hook can sink through and make way for the next row of stitches. However, it is dull enough to keep the yarn from severing or fraying. Different hooks will have slightly different tip shapes and sharpness levels, but they all have unique uses.

The throat of crochet needles can vary greatly. The size of an individual crochet needle's throat is determined by the projected type of yarn that will be used with that type of needle. Needles with larger throats are intended to be used with yarn that has a heavier weight. Alternatively, needles with smaller throats will be used with yarn that has lighter weight. Intermediate needles will be used with intermediately-weighted yarns. For instance, a needle with a throat diameter of four millimeters is generally used with DK, or light, yarn. Some throats are particularly sharp, and some are rounded. It is a matter of preference for the most part, but make sure you do not get a needle with a throat that is too sharp, or it may fray your yarn. As long as you have durable yarn, it should not be much of a problem if you go with a sharper hook. However, it is always a good idea to test out the hook on a small section of your yarn to make sure that it will not fray before you use it for a big project.

The shank of the crochet hook is the longest part of your hook, and your loops of the thread will reside there while you crochet your rows and rounds. The length of the shank of your hook gives you a good idea of how long the rows of your pattern will be, for if you have a longer shank, you have the potential to make a long row of stitches and chains. Try to opt for a longer crochet hook with a reasonably sized shank so you can have wiggle room for the length of your project. The shank can also determine how large or small your individual stitches will be due to the diameter of the hook itself.

The grip and handle are where you will be holding your crochet hook. The grip, which is sometimes called the thumb rest, is a relatively flat section of the hook that you hold with your thumb and index finger whilst crocheting your piece. The thumb rest, or grip, of the crochet hook, is a very ergonomic inclusion to the hook that allows you to easily turn and manipulate it as you create chains and stitches. The handle is where the bottommost part of your hand rests when you hold onto the crochet hook. Both are important for stabilizing the hook and ensuring the best level of control over your crocheting techniques.

Another important note that you should consider when purchasing a crochet hook is the way the sloping of the shank to the point area is made. If there is a particularly angular slope from the point to the shank, it can make crocheting smoothly a fairly difficult task. If it is a fluid and gradual slope, it will be much easier to maneuver the yarn onto the hook, and the yarn will glide much more smoothly up the hook. Make sure you also avoid a hook with no slope, as it will be increasingly difficult to get the yarn onto the hook at all in this case. When you have no slope, the point of the hook is too wide, and it prevents the normal ease of sliding the yarn onto your hook. This slope also affects the size and width of your stitches, so it is important to keep that in mind as well.

Now that you know all that you could possibly need to know about hooks, consider which varieties would be beneficial to your style, comfort, and planned crocheting patterns. There are so many types of hook that you can spend hours searching for the correct one, but if you go into it with a general idea, it will be much easier to choose the right one. Every individual has a different set of preferences, so go with what is most comfortable for you and what fits into your preferred crocheting style and yarn types.

Browse your local stores to try out the different hook types, and sure are sure to find something that will be perfect for you!

**Yarn**

Yarn is the most important material you will need when you crochet, for yarn is what your projects will be made of! You can't crochet without yarn, so you'd better fill the majority of your crocheting toolbox with it! Later in this chapter, we will discuss the many varieties of yarn so that you can pick the best ones for you and your project. You can get yarn in any color, consistency, thickness, texture, or durability that you want! You just have to shop around a bit and read this chapter to figure out which ones suit your preferences.

You can buy yarn in many retail stores, specialty stores, craft stores, and more! There are online retailers as well, and your possibilities are nearly endless. The Yarn is sold in a few different ways. Normally, you find yarn in skeins, or hanks, and balls, and they are generally bound by a label that describes its properties such as yardage, weight, material percentages, and the like. It also gives instructions for washing the products you make from the yarn and the suggested size of the hooks. Try to save this label, so you don't forget the aspects of your yarn once you start using it. It can also help to keep the label with what you make from the yarn, so you remember how to wash it and how to make similar items in the future.

The weight of your yarn, which we will analyze deeply later in this chapter, factors into the number of stitches and rows, will be needed for your pattern. You will need bigger hooks for heavier yarn and smaller hooks for lighter yarn. Heavier yarn normally needs less overall stitches and takes less time to complete a project. Heavy yarn makes coarser and bulky products, which has a nice and comfy aesthetic. Lighter yarn is used for lacier projects and decorations, and it can be used much more intricately.

If you purchase yarn in a hank or skein instead of a ball, make sure to roll the yarn into a manageable ball to prevent tangles if you would like an easier task. It will help you in the long run, though it may take a bit of time until you get used to it. You can do this by hand or with a special device called a ball winder.

When you begin shopping for yarn, factor in the resilience, durability, loft, feel washability, and more to get a good idea about what you will be working with. Make sure you get yarn that fits your preferences and lifestyle and go for the levels that work for you. The comfort is also a factor, so make sure to get something as soft as you prefer, that can retain heat, and more. Bear in mind that fuzzier yarn tends to lose its shape easier, and it is not as adaptable to washing.

## Scissors

Scissors are a common crochet tool that you will use when snipping excess yarn and switching between colors in a pattern. You use scissors to finish off your projects and snip the yarn that is to be fastened at the end of the pattern. Make sure to pick up a nice, sharp pair of sewing scissors before you begin crocheting so you will never be without this important tool. If they are too dull, it will fray the yarn and make it harder to fasten it off completely.

## Tapestry Needles

Tapestry needles are important for those wishing to do crochet. When you crochet a complex pattern with many parts, you often need to sew those parts together. You also need to use a tapestry needle to fasten off a finished piece. For instance, if you crochet a bag with handles, you will need to sew those handles onto the body of the bag with a tapestry needle. You will also need them when attaching pom-poms to beanies and similar projects. When in doubt, bring a tapestry needle with you just in case you will need to sew your project together. More often than not, you will need it.

Make sure that you get a tapestry needle that is sharp enough to pierce the yarn so you can sew into it but blunt enough to not fray or damage the yarn itself. Most tapestry needles are manufactured to be the right level of bluntness, but always check to make sure. Aim for a needle that is as small as you can get in accordance with the yarn you are using, and try to sew with the same yarn type that you used in your piece to get a clean look. I would also like to advise against plastic tapestry needles, as they do not work as well as other materials. They do not slide enough through the yarn, and they are not slippery enough to do the job as well as is needed.

**Tape Measure**

Tape measures are quite useful when doing any craft, but they are particularly useful for crochet. Tape measures can help you measure yourself and your friends to make sure that the things you make for them will fit perfectly. Tape measures are also a great way to make sure your patterns are on track, for it can help you count and measure the rows of your project. Make sure to keep a tape measure handy for any of your more ambitious projects so you can always stay on track.

**Safety Pins**

Safety pins are great for helping you keep your place when you crochet. They will help you remember which row you are on, serve as a marker for your projects, and more. Keep a handful of safety pins by your work station or in a nearby drawer in case you need them for a project. They will really come in handy! You can fasten the loose ends of your stitches, keep your place, and use pins for a wide variety of instances while crocheting. You can even hold certain rows of stitches together so you. They are incredibly beneficial to have on hand with almost any project.

**Cardboard Cutouts**

Cardboard cutouts are useful for maintaining the shape of whatever project you are working on. You can crochet around these cutouts or use them to stabilize a hollow piece that you are creating. They have many uses, so make sure to keep some around for whenever you start doing three-dimensional crochet projects!

## Pom-pom Circles

Pom-poms are a nice additive to many projects, such as hats, gloves, and more. Keep a few pom-pom circles handy, so you can add creative flair to your projects! They are quite fluffy, and they are great for kid projects and other cute pieces. They are particularly great with wintry projects, and you really can't go wrong with these cute puffs of fluff!

## Decorations or Embellishments

Things like buttons, beads, colorful ribbons, and other embellishments add flair and personality to your projects. It's a good thing to keep a fair supply of beads, ribbons, and buttons around in case you would like to decorate your crochet projects. Some examples of this include beaded crochet, adding buttons to baby hats and other clothing items, and incorporating ribbons into gorgeous decorated pieces. If you want to add decorative designs to your crochet projects, embellishments are the way to go.

## Row Counter

Row counters are invaluable when you start to crochet. They will help you keep your place when you are working on a project, and they genuinely help you stay on the right track, so you don't get lost between the rows. Essentially, row counters are little chains that you loop onto your crochet hook and have little numbers on them that you can move to track your row progress while working. After every row, you move up to the next number in the chain, so you don't lose your progress.

## A Calm, Perfect Crocheting Location

Arguably, the most important thing you can have for your crocheting experience is the perfect workspace. There's nothing better than a comfortable, quiet place to sit and crochet, and it is different for everyone! Some may like to sit in a well-lit sunroom with birds chirping outside. Others prefer to sit on the couch and crochet mindlessly while watching their favorite TV shows. There are even those who like to relax in bed and crochet under the warm covers! There is no wrong answer here, and anywhere can be your crocheting sanctuary if you want it to be! Just find a place where you are comfortable and where you enjoy crocheting, and it will be perfect.

**Types of Yarn**

## Yarn Weight

Yarn weight pertains to the thickness of each strand of the yarn. It does not necessarily have to do with the weight of the yarn in ounces, grams, or pounds, but it is a common term for those who seek out certain thicknesses of yarn. The smallest of these are lace yarn, and the largest of these are jumbo yarn. We will go over each of the yarn weight types in this chapter so you can determine which types, if not all types, you would like to include in your crocheting toolbox.

From thinnest and lightest to the heaviest and thickest in composition, here is a list of the yarn weight types:

- Lace
- Super Fine
- Fine
- Light
- Medium
- Bulky
- Super Bulky
- Jumbo

Make sure to pay attention to your yarn weights when you decide on what project you would like to make next. Many yarns are great for one thing but not so great for another. For instance, you would not likely use a jumbo yarn for something as small as a coaster, and you would not use a superfine yarn for a warm, comfy blanket. You could, in theory, use whatever yarn you would like, but the results you get will change drastically depending on the weight of the yarn. When in doubt, read the description on the yarn packaging or label to get a good idea of what each type is generally used for.

Generally, the small yarn weights like lace, super fine, and fine are used to make lightweight shawls and scarves, doilies, and decorative crafts. The Jumbo yarn is unique in that you can use it to do arm-crocheting. Its giant size makes it great for blankets. The Yarns that fall in the middle can be used for a wide variety of projects. Just use your noggin and justify how thick or think you'd like your projects to be, and go from there when you purchase your yarn.

Also, bear in mind that there are specific hook sizes that you will need to use for each range of yarn weights. Your standard hook will likely do well with most of the middle-ground and lower yarn weights, but yarns such as those in the jumbo category need a much larger hook than your everyday crochet hook.

**Yarn Materials**

There are many types of fibers and materials that are used to make yarn. For the most part, the yarn material you use is based on personal preference. The most popular, in general, is cotton, but there are many natural and synthetic fibers out there today. There are synthetic yarns, which are man-made, as well as plant-based and animal-based. Finding the right yarn is incredibly important, for certain yarns work better for the different types of projects you will make. For instance, softer yarns are great for sweaters and hats; coarse yarn is great for bags, and so forth.

Make sure you pick the right type of yarn for you, but above all, experiment and have fun with it! Let's see what the material types are!

***Plant-Based:***

- Bamboo – Bamboo is a less common yarn, but it has great properties! Bamboo has been known to carry antibacterial properties, and it is very pretty when the yarn fibers create a soft, draping look to whatever you make out of them. This lightweight, breathable yarn is perfect for summer garments and anything that looks pretty with a draping aesthetic. Shawls, light blankets, and decorations look lovely when made with bamboo yarn. Some even say that bamboo yarn is softer than silk and that it wears very well.

- Cotton – Cotton is a very popular type of yarn, if not the most popular. It is made from natural cotton fibers and is great to use in almost any crocheting project. It is a very good beginner yarn, and it is suitable for any level of crocheting hobbyists. Cotton is loved for its durability, breathability, and availability! It is very absorbent as well. Cotton is great for creating any type of clothing, and it's a great material to use when crocheting just about anything. The only downside to cotton is that it does not always hold its shape, but its benefits outweigh the negatives.

- Hemp – Hemp is a fairly new type of yarn, and it is made from the hemp plant. It is used most often for knitting socks, sweaters, and warm-weather clothing, but it can be used for anything you set your mind to! Hemp fiber is surprisingly soft, and it is fairly cheap due to the high production rate of the hemp plant. The hemp plant produces over two times as much fiber as the cotton plant, which is great for us! Hemp is also hypoallergenic, antibacterial, and resists fungal growth. It holds up very well in the washer machine and the dryer, and it does not shrink or lose its shape! As an added bonus, it actually gets softer when you wash it. It is incredibly durable, breathable and it protects against UV radiation. This well-rounded fiber is great for anyone who would like a natural crochet yarn.

- Linen – Linen is made from flax. More specifically, it is created by extracting the fibers of the flax plant's stem, deep within the core of the stem, and past the bark. Linen is a great type of fiber to work with, especially in yarn, for it is stronger than cotton and lasts much longer than other types of yarn. It is, however, not as soft as animal fibers and cotton, as it is a bit rougher, but it is a great type of yarn to use for decorative projects and clothing items suited for warmer weather.

*Synthetic*:

- Acrylic – Acrylic yarn is man-made and often referred to as microfiber. It is relatively cheap to purchase and is popular among beginners. It is often mixed with either wool or cotton, and it is quite easy to find on the market. Acrylic works well in braided patterns, crocheted rugs, and more.
- Faux-fur – These strings of synthetic fibers are made to look and feel like fur. Faux-fur yarn is less expensive than animal-fiber yarn,

though it can be just as fluffy. It is mostly created with nylon, but it can be made with other materials as well. If you want something that looks like fur, but you don't want to spend a lot of money, this is a good option. This type of yarn is known as a novelty yarn due to its unique style and comparability to wool.

- Nylon – Nylon is rarely used on its own, but it is often added to cotton yarn, acrylic yarn, and wool-blended yarn to give it a bit more durability and strength. It is often used when crocheting socks, gloves, and similarly small items. It is not very common as a yarn unless it is blended with other materials, but it is quite durable and holds its shape well. It is also incredibly easy to wash.

- Polyester – Polyester yarn includes a blend of plant-based and animal-based fibers. Normally, it is made with cotton and sheep's wool, and it is used to create many types of novelty yarns. It is a bit bulkier than other yarns, but it is useful if you want a unique spin to your crocheting game. Polyester yarn is used to make glow-in-the-dark yarn, ribbon yarn, and various other yarn types. It is known as one of the most difficult yarns to work with for beginners due to the way it twists when you use it, but it can be fun with a bit of practice.

## *Animal-Based:*

- Wool in General – All of the materials in this list are wool types, as wool is any type of fiber obtained from the fur of animals. Wool is known as the most sought-after yarn material, as it is incredibly durable, soft, and wonderful at insulating heat. Wool is normally the number one choice of yarn for new and seasoned crafters due to its popularity and usability. Every type of wool has its own characteristics and benefits, but for the most part, wool is the best yarn type you can get if you don't mind animal fibers.

- Alpaca – Alpaca yarn is made from the fur of an animal called an alpaca. It can be a bit tricky to maneuver if you are a beginner, but it is incredibly soft and fluffy. It is widely used in sweaters, teddy bears, and common clothing items. Alpaca yarn comes in two varieties, depending on how it is spun. It can be either lightweight or heavy, so make sure to pay attention to the weight of the yarn when you purchase it to make sure it is the variety that you would like. Alpaca is a wonderful yarn type to use, for it is hypoallergenic, water-resistant, and incredibly soft. If you love the softness of animal fibers but are prone to allergies, this could be the perfect yarn for you! When caring for this type of yarn, however, make sure to avoid throwing it in the washing machine. It loses its shape very easily, so try to hand wash gently it whenever it needs to be washed.

- Angora – Angora wool is made from the fur of fuzzy Angora rabbits. It is quite lightweight, but it retains a lovely amount of warmth and softness. It is silky and soft in texture, and it has many benefits for the skin. It has been said that Angora wool, and therefore Angora yarn, improves circulation and retains warmth three times better than other types of wool. The warmth and airiness of Angora yarn lead to improvements in the skin's temperature, arthritis patients, sciatica, muscle issues, cold joints, and more. It is among the fluffiest of all yarn types, the mist lightweight, and the warmest! It is perfect for sweaters, socks, gloves, blankets, and more! It is said that angora wool floats like a cloud, pertaining to how light and fluffy it is to wear. I cannot say many negative things about this yarn type, as it is simply a wonderful type of yarn to use.

- Cashmere – Cashmere, similar to mohair, is made from the back and shoulder fur of goats. This specific fur is harvested from cashmere goats, and it is the soft and fuzzy undercoat of these creatures that are used for wool production. Cashmere is very smooth and silky, and it is incredibly soft to the touch. In fact, it is one of the softest yarns you can find. It can be a bit pricey, as many high-end clothing items are made from cashmere wool, but it is certainly worth the price. It is particularly expensive due to the process that is used to harvest the wool. Most goats only produce a small amount of fiber, so it is a laborious process. In ancient times, cashmere was used to clothe royalty, but today, you can have warm cashmere clothing too! All you have to do is crochet it. The only downside to cashmere is that it is less strong than sheep wool due to how soft it is, but it should last for quite some time as long as you take good care of it.

- Llama – Llama yarn comes from the fur of the llama. This type of yarn is hypoallergenic and quite warm, used to make sweaters, scarves, and much more. This lightweight yarn is a lot like that of the alpaca, offering a lot of warmth without heavyweight. It provides many lovely natural colors, and it does not shrink in the washer. It can lose its shape if you wash it too often, but as long as you wash it in cold water on a gentle cycle, it should be fine. This is a great type of yarn for those who like a lightweight, soft, and warm alternative to alpaca and other types of yarns.

- Merino – Merino yarn comes from the wool of Merino sheep. These sheep grow Merino wool all year long, and they produce a quality product due to the amiable living qualities they reside in. They are normally given plenty of fresh air, ample amounts of grass to munch on, are well-hydrated, and get plenty of sunshine. These all lead to a happy sheep and lots of quality wool production. The wool is arguably the most ancient and well-known type of animal fiber known to man, as it has been used for centuries. This type of yarn is quite easy to wash and care for, and it is loved by those who crochet. It is among the warmest and softest of wool types, and it is very popular. Merino yarn, much like alpaca yarn, is hypoallergenic and great for cold-weather clothing. Unlike alpaca yarn, however, Merino yarn holds its shape very well.

- Mohair – Mohair is a fancy way of saying goat hair. Mohair yarn is made from the soft fur of goats, and it is most frequently harvested from Angora goats. Mohair yarn has a nice sheen to it, and it is very durable. It is often incorporated into yarn mixtures to make them stronger and easier to use, but pure mohair yarn is where it shines the best. Mohair yarn is unique in that it has great moisture-absorbing abilities. It is great when used in rugs, coasters, and even clothing! It will hold up quite well over the years and offer comfort and durability. Due to its ability to withstand the elements, this type of yarn can be rather expensive. If you want long-lasting, durable clothing, however, this is a great choice. The only downside apart from the price is that mohair yarn can be a bit itchy to some people.
- Silk – Silk is made from the fibers that silkworms and other insects create naturally. Their webs, cocoons, or other naturally made creations are collected and harvested for their silk threads. Those threads are then woven and manufactured into the fabric, yarn, and more. Silk yarn is very sleek and smooth, and it is quite pleasing to the touch. It is used in many clothing items and similar products like shirts, pillowcases, and more. Despite its fairly slippery nature, silk yarn is pretty easy to work with. It does not catch as much as other materials, and it is a lovely way to make warm-weather pieces of clothing. Silk yarn is one of the most expensive types of yarn you can purchase due to the fact that it is the strongest of all-natural fibers, and it takes a while to harvest and process the silk.

## Yarn Color

Yarn comes in a large variety of color patterns. You can find yarn in nearly every color of the rainbow, but the consistency and visibility of the colors depend on the coloring type that you choose in your yarn. The eight types of yarn coloring include:

- Solid – Normally, solid-color yarn is a singular, bright color that is easy to distinguish.
- Blended – Blended-color yarn is a blend of two or more colors.
- Rainbow – Rainbow yarn includes a compilation of many different colors. Normally the iconic colors of the rainbow are represented.
- Novelty – Novelty yarn colors can be bizarre, such as glow-in-the-dark varieties, and they are often chosen for their unique look and fun design potential.
- Heather – Heather colors are made of two or so different colors combined to make a unique hue. They often have flecks of other colors that give the yarn a nice blended look.
- Tweed – Tweed yarn normally has solid, earthy colors with specs of other colors incorporated into it.
- Marbled – Marbled yarn is similar to a rainbow, but it is normally only two or three colors that are swirled or blended together to make a pretty transition between hues.

# Chapter 2. Simple Stitches and Techniques

## Slip Stitch

Use this to join your chain stitch together in preparation for forming a ring. Many believe that this is the easiest of the stitches that you will learn, and it is definitely a basic stitch. All you have to do is pick up the yarn and loop it over the hook, which is called a yarn over, and pass your hook through a stitch to pick the yarn up. Once you do this, bring the hook back through the same stitch and the stitch that is on the hook in one fluid sweep. That's all there is to it!

## Slipstitch

Do not be fooled. The slipstitch is not the slip stitch. The slipstitch is a technique in which you combine two layers of fabric, as with a lining and an outer fabric. It can work in a number of ways, but at its core, it basically is the process in which you slip a stitch between a lining and an outer layer of fabric in order to combine them. Take your thread and place it in the outer layer of the project on the right-hand side. Then, bring up the needle until it is in the fold of the lining. Once it is in the lining, take it into the outer fabric directly above the lining and take it back up and through the fabric repeatedly without going all the way through to the outside of the fabric.

With a slipstitch, the stitches should be as tiny as you can get them and as close together as you can make them, depending on the size of the project.

The bigger the project, the more widely spaced they can be, but generally, you want to keep them fairly close together.

## Chain Stitch

This is a very simple stitch and the one that most people learn first. Most, if not all, projects begin with a chain stitch. Normally, you use the chain stitch to build up the foundation of your project and get the ball rolling. You work it from right to left and bring the needle or hook up through the starting point to make a loop in the fabric. Then, you take the needle back down to where it came from to complete it. Then, you hold the loop with your fingers and bring the hookup, then over the loop, and finally pull it back through the loop to secure it. You repeat as needed for the distance you require, and the loop sizes depend entirely on your project.

## Single Crochet Stitch

This is one of the easiest crochet stitches you can learn, and it is not hard at all to master. It is in many basic patterns and projects, so you will be using it often. Start by passing your hook through your previous row's stitch. Do this by passing the hook under the front of the loop and the back, then onto the top of the stitch. Pick your yarn back up after that and pull it back through until you end with two loops remaining on the hook. Once you are at this point, hook the yarn onto your crochet hook and bring it through the two loops simultaneously. One of these loops should remain on your hook once this is complete, and this is the point at which your single crochet stitch is finished.

## Half-Double Crochet Stitch

This is an intermediate stitch that is present in many crochet patterns. It is not as difficult as it sounds, and it will definitely come in handy during your projects. Twirl your yarn around the hook one time to start. Then, pass the hook up through the stitch that you are going to be working into.

Hook your yarn now before bringing it back through the stitches. You should have three hoops on your crochet hook now. This will include the original stitches loop, the loop you made prior to inserting your hook, and your currently picked-up loop. Confirm that you have these three loops, then hook your yarn once more. Draw the hook through the three loops you have acquired. You should have one hoop on your hook now. You should now have a completed half-double crochet stitch if you have followed every step. That's it!

## Double Crochet Stitch

The double crochet stitch has many uses in crocheting, and it is known as the unlimited-use stitch. To begin this stitch, twirl the yarn once around the hook. Then, slide the hook through the stitch with which you are going to work. Hook the yarn with your crochet hook and swiftly pulls it back through the stitch.

By now, you should have a total of three loops on the length of your crochet hook. The loops should include the starting stitch's loop, the loop you made before you inserted your crochet hook, and the loop you picked up just now. Make sure you have these three loops, then proceed.

Hook your yarn once more unto your crochet hook before drawing it back through the first two of your loops. Do this again, but pass it through the two hooks that remain on your hook. The stitch will be complete when you see one double crochet below your hook and one loop remaining at the end of your crochet hook.

## Triple Crochet Stitch

This stitch is the embodiment of doing a yarn over twice a tactic. Basically, you start by twirling the yarn over your hook twice, as the tactic suggests. Then, you pass the hook through the stitch with which you will be working. Once you have this finished, hook your yarn and bring it through the stitch you've just passed through. If you have done this correctly, you should have four loops total on the length of your hook.

The four loops should include the one from your starting stitch, two from the double-twirled yarn, and one from the loop you just picked up by coming back through your stitch. Once you are sure you have all four loops, hook your yarn once more and draw it back through the first two of your loops.

Do this again, but bring it through the second pair of loops. To finish it off, hook your yarn and pass it back through the remaining two loops on your crochet hook. Your triple crochet stitch should now be complete, and one loop should remain on the hook.

## Double Triple Crochet Stitch

The double triple crochet stitch starts similarly to the triple crochet stitch, but instead of wrapping the yarn around the hook twice, you will do this three times. Then, you pass the hook through the stitch you will be working into. Next, hook your yarn and pull it back through your stitch.

Now you should have five total loops on the length of your crochet hook. After ensuring that this is correct, hook your yarn once more and pull it back through the first two loops on the crochet hook. You should now have four loops in total.

Next, hook your yarn once more and pass it through the second pair of loops on the crochet hook. Do this one more time and pass the hook through the third pair of loops before hooking the yarn and bringing through the final pair of loops on the hook. You should be left with one loop on the hook when this is done, and you will have a completed double triple crochet stitch below.

## Overcasting

Overcasting is a stitching method used to finish what is called a raw edge. You can vary it to join two sections of a project, or you can use it to pull raw edges together in a way that makes them as imperceptibly as possible. You generally work from the left side to the right and use tiny, vertical stitches to create an overcasting stitch pattern. You pull the stitches through both sections of the raw edge and pull them very tightly together to get as invisible of a stitch as you can achieve.

# Chapter 3. Stitch Variations

Simple stitch variations like the ones below are a great way to change up your crochet patterns and spice them up with your personality. They can completely change the aesthetic of mundane pieces and wow your friends and family. Try them out for yourself and see!

## Back Loop Stitch

To make a back loop, you ignore the loops at the top of the stitch that you would normally insert the crochet hook into. Instead, go under the back loop of the stitch and work into the stitch that way. The back loop is farthest from you on the piece, and it is normally not the loop that is closest to the wrong side of the piece.

Next, finish the row as you would, but use the back loop instead of the normal insertion point of each stitch. This will give you a nice texture to your piece. Once you work a few rows this way, you will begin to see a ridged pattern form. In fact, another name for this stitching variation is horizontal ribbing, but it is normally only used with single crochet stitches.

## Front Loop Stitch

Front loop stitches are similar to back loop stitches, but instead of working through the back loop, you go through the front loop. This technique, rather than giving a ribbed look like with back loop stitching, gives the piece a fluid, lacy look that drapes rather nicely. The front loop that you are working with is the loop that is closest to you in the piece. As you work these stitches, finish the row by inserting the hook into only the front loop stitches.

## Extended Stitch

Extended stitches are longer than normal crochet stitches, and they are taller as well. They give a much looser look to the piece, and they are created by adding an extra yarnover to work. The stitches incorporated through the extended stitch create a flexible, easy-to-drape fabric. They are often used to shape corners and lessen the possibility of taut edges. Other names for the extended stitch include the Elmore stitch and the locked stitch.

To work an extended stitch, start by making the stitches normally. Then, hook your crochet hook into each stitch, then wrap your yarn over and around the hook before drawing the loop back through the front of the piece. Next, repeat the process of wrapping the yarn over and pull it through a single loop that rests on the hook. That completes the yarn that you need to make the extended stitch, and you are left with the same number of stitches on your hook. Finish the stitches normally before wrapping your yarn over the hook one more time and pull it through the two loops that remain on the hook.

# Chapter 4. Relief Stitches and Raised Stitches

Raised and relief stitches, also referred to as post stitches, are created when you inject your crochet hook around the post of your stitch below rather than inserting it under the topmost loops of the stitch. You normally do this with taller stitches, as with double crochet stitches. It gives your pieces nice textural patterns, and it can set them apart from more mundane pieces. Make your projects your own by trying a few of these varieties out for yourself!

## Front Post Stitch

The front post stitch is created in tandem with double crochet stitches. To begin, wrap your yarn over your crochet hook a single time. Then, work from the front of your crochet pattern and inject the hook, bringing it around the post of the stitch that is below the row you are working on. Work right to left, then bring the hook back through to the front of the piece. After you do this, wrap your yarn back over the hook and bring a loop through. Finish by completing a normal double crochet stitch.

## Back Post Stitch

As with the front post stitch, you will be using double crochet to incorporate your back post stitches. Wrap your yarn over your crochet hook a single time. Then, work from the back of your project and insert your hook through the front and bring it around the post of your stitch below. Work from right to left, then bring your hook back through the back of the project. Wrap the yarn around your crochet hook once more, then finish your double crochet stitch normally.

## Raised Rib Stitching

Raised rib stitching is accomplished by merging back and front post stitches. It makes a flexible rib that works great on the sleeves of many garments. You create this by evenly making a foundation chain, creating a chain plus two. Then, you do one double crochet in the fourth chain from your hook. Then do one double crochet in each chain to the end of the row. After that, turn your piece and chain two. Skip your first double crochet and do one front post stitch in the next double crochet stitch. Then, do one back post stitch in the double crochet that follows. Repeat this to the end of the row. Turn your piece and repeat the process for the remainder of the pattern, turning the piece after every additional row of stitches.

## Basketweave Stitching

A basketweave stitching pattern gives a lovely aesthetic to your piece, and it is also created with back and front post stitches. You work sections of the front and back post stitches down each row, and it can be used for blankets, scarves, pillows, and similar items. Repeat the process as many times as you need to get your desired width and length for your piece. This process uses quite a bit of yarn, but it is worth it!

## Crossed Stitch

For a crossed stitch, you normally go off a specific pattern to make the stitch. With this type of stitch, you do not work into the next stitch in the normal way. You insert the hook, rather, into a specified place in the pattern of the piece. For instance, you could work the crossed stitch into the four or five stitches to the right of your supposed next stitch. Then, work the stitch in a normal way by drawing the loop through your fabric and up through to the same height as nearby stitches. Bring your yarn up to meet the height of the other stitches to ensure fluidity among the stitches. Continue the row as normal after this.

## Spike Stitch

A spiked stitch, or dropped stitch, creates a nice, compact texture that goes nicely with a complementary color from the main piece. They are used, often with more than one color, to make interesting striped designs in your project. You use a single crochet to create them, and you insert the hook into a row below the one you are working on to give a little spice to your design. You use a longer loop in order to make the yarn reach the lower row while you make the stitch in order to avoid a stitch that is too tight. You wouldn't want to squish your stitches! You can make quite a few spiked stitches in a single stitch to make striking spiked designs, and it looks particularly nice when you use colors that complement or contrast the main color of the piece.

First, put your hook from the front to the back into a row below the one you are working on. Then, wrap your yarn up and over your crochet hook before drawing through a loop. Make the loop large enough to stretch down to the lower row without squishing your stitches. Then, complete your stitch in a normal fashion.

# Chapter 5. Techniques

## How to Crochet for Right-Handers

Before we look at patterns, we need to study the fundamentals of crocheting, which start with how to hold the yarn. In this chapter, we will teach you not only how to crochet according to patterns, but also how to hold yarn, how to make knots, and so on.

## How to Hold the Yarn

One of the first things you must learn is how to hold your yarn properly. This comes before learning to secure the yarn on the crochet hook. Holding the yarn may differ depending on whether you are right-handed or left-handed. If you are a right-hander, your left hand will be your yarn hand, and your right hand will be the one that holds the crochet hook.

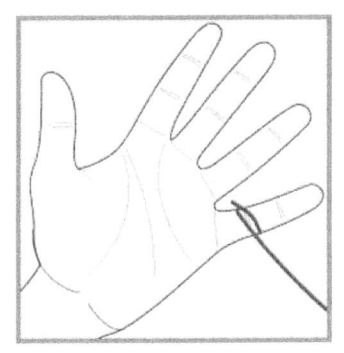

To begin, use your left hand and bring the yarn between your little finger and ring finger and wrap it just once, making a loop around the bottom little finger.

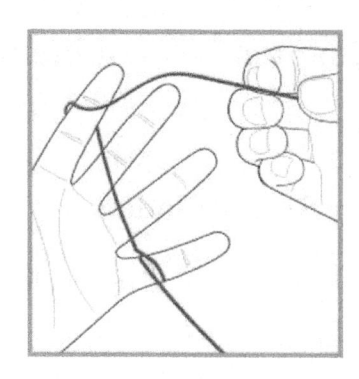

Next, move the yarn across diagonally on the inside of your hand. Then, make another loop on your ring finger by bringing it to the top of the index finger and looping it to the inside of the finger.

Next, create a slip knot. A slip knot is used to keep the yarn in place. This will give you greater control while stitching.

Firstly, lay your yarn down flat on the table. Take about six inches from the end of the yarn and create a loop that looks like a pretzel.

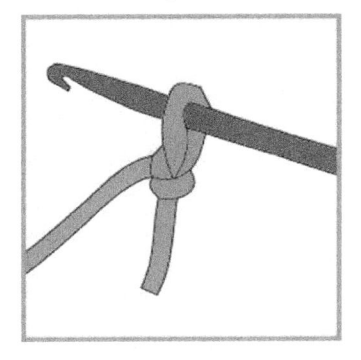

Next, hold the loop with your left hand and then move your crochet hook through the center of it, as seen in the image.

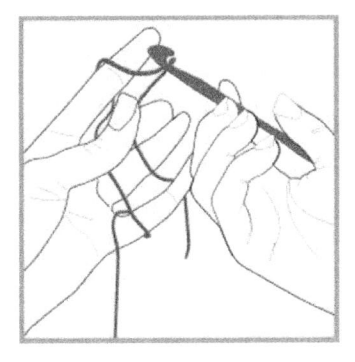

Next, tighten the loop around the hook by gently pulling both ends of the yarn. Allow a little allowance. Here, your slip knot should easily slide up and down the shaft of your hook, but it should be firm enough not to come off over the end.

Using your middle finger and thumb to keep the yarn in place, clasp the yarn with your fingers and hold the crochet hook in your other hand. Holding your hook and yarn in this manner provides plenty of room for you to maneuver, and it also helps you control the yarn's tension by either lowering or raising your index finger.

## How to Crochet for Left-handers

For the left-handed crafters out there, you are well aware of how confusing it can be to follow right-handed methods and adjust them to suit your needs. Crochet patterns and instructions are made for right-handers unless otherwise mentioned.

There are so few left-handed crafters and being a minority, there are not many sources available to learn from. This is because only a small percentage of people are left-handed and most of them are men. So, when it comes to doing crafts, particularly crafts for women, instructions for left-handers are not a priority.

Most left-handed women use right-handed instructional tools and prefer to use those. They end up learning how to crochet with their right hand. This may be alright for some, whereas others don't have as much coordination in their right hand to create a smooth rhythm. It is also possible to follow right-handed instructions and adjust them accordingly so that you can use your left hand to crochet. This can work but it is confusing at times, and one needs to concentrate carefully.

So, if you are a lefty and you intend to take up crochet as a hobby, this guide should be very useful and hopefully make the process a lot easier for you.

Let's Get Started!

The most important thing is to get a firm and comfortable grip on your crochet hook as this will allow you to proceed to the next step. So, once you have a grip on it with your left hand, you'll need to use your right hand for holding the yarn. This is simply the opposite of what right-handers do. You choose, as right-handers do, to hold your crochet hook using your thumb and your index finger to keep it in place, or you can simply grip it as you would a knife. Both ways are easy to get used to, so just decide which one you prefer using and learn to crochet that way.

There are, of course, several ways that you can hold your yarn as you work your stitches and that is up to you. One of the most commonly used methods is to loop the yarn using your right index finger. Keep the loose end up and then allow the thread that is attached to the yarn to lie on your palm in a cross manner. Once you have done this, you can use the free end of the yarn to create a slip knot to start the crochet process.

Once you have done that, using your right hand, then hold the slip knot you have made between your fingers' middle and thumb. This is the most comfortable position for this. Your yarn will be between your index finger and your thumb, so you'll be able to control your tension nicely using your index finger. Controlling your tension will help you to create consistent, even stitches. It is best to master this from the beginning as it will make a huge difference to the quality of your work later on.

## What Is the Difference Between Right and Left-Handed Crafters?

- Although it is confusing to change hands when crocheting, the main differences between right-handed and left-handed techniques are as follows:
- You either grip your crochet hook in your right or left hand.
- You'll hold the yarn in your free hand.
- The direction you work in changes as a left-hander as you'll work your stitches from left to right, whereas a right-hander will do the opposite.
- To work the stitches in rounds, left-handers will work in a counter-clockwise direction to the right. Right-handers will do the opposite and work their stitches in a clockwise direction to the left.
- Crochet rounds worked by left-handers have a different appearance compared to those made by right-handers. Although some right-handed crocheters think that left-handers' rounds look odd, others actually prefer them.
- Rows worked by left-handers look the same as those done by right-handers, except that the yarn has been fastened off on the other end, so that is the only difference.
- Once you start, you'll have a piece of yarn that hangs down. This is your yarn tail. Always leave the tail hanging and never crochet over it. If a pattern has a right side and a wrong side of the work, your tail can be used to give you a hint. When the tail is hanging

on the bottom right-hand corner, and then that makes it the right side to work on.

- Each time that you do the yarning over, you will pick up the yarn in a clockwise direction. This is a good point to remember at all times.

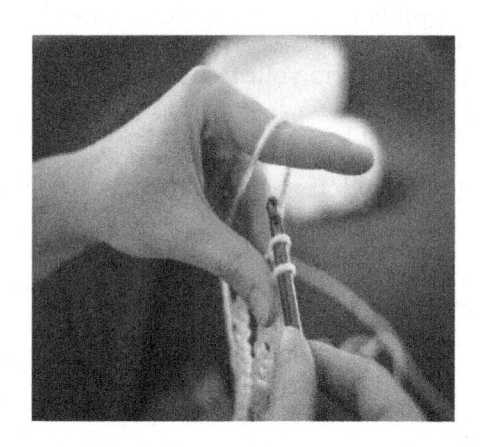

## How to Hold Hook and Yarn

Holding your hook and yarn may seem like a pretty simple task, but you have to know how to do it precisely before starting any of your crocheting techniques. If you do not hold your hook and yarn correctly, it will hinder any and all stitches and techniques you try to use. Not to worry, however, for I will tell you just how to hold your materials so you can create your crocheting masterpieces with ease!

Though I stressed that holding your hook and yarn is incredibly important, it is a matter of preference how you specifically choose to hold it. As long as you follow this basic practice of holding them, you will be ok. From there, you can adjust it to your preferences.

To begin, you will want to hold the hook similar to how you would hold a carving knife. You can hold the hook down and rest your thumb on the hook while securing it with your pointer finger. Then, wrap your other fingers around the hook to loosely but securely hold it all in place. The looseness helps you adjust your grip, and the stabilization keeps the hook in a good position for adding stitches and performing your crochet techniques.

You can also hold the hook much like you would hold a pencil as long as you keep it secure, and it is natural in your hand. You want to keep your hand comfortable while securing the hook and allowing it to maneuver with the yarn as best as it can. Once you have your hook-hand situated, you can focus on the yarn.

Depending on your dominant hand, you can hold the hook in either. It is preferred to hold the hook in your dominant hand, so if you are right-handed, hold it in your right hand. If you are left-handed, you can hold it in your left hand. Again, this is a matter of preference, but it is easier to hold the hook with your dominant hand.

Now, let's talk about yarn. It is generally best to hold your yarn in your non-dominant hand, but regardless of the hand when you hold your yarn, you want to focus on controlling the tension of the yarn. Wind the yarn around your fingers smoothly to ensure that you can slide it through your fingers and increase the tightness or looseness of it. Make sure you keep it at a tension level where it can run through your fingers well but not be so loose that you lose control of it. Generally, you will want to separate your index finger from your next three fingers. Then, place the yarn across the top of your pinky, ring, and middle fingers. Slide it down to the bottom of these fingers and secure the yarn with your pinky. Once you do that, loop the yarn across the top of your ring and middle fingers, and you're ready to crochet!

**Steps to a slipknot**

To start almost any crochet project, you will need to make a slipknot. You will need to follow several very easy steps.

You will begin all crochet work with a slipknot. It acts as the first stitch that you make as well as an anchor point so that your yarn does not unravel as you work. You can tighten or loosen this knot rather easily, making it versatile. You will need to follow the steps as seen below.

The first step demonstrates making the loop. Place it fifteen centimeters (3 inches) from the end of the yarn to make sure that you have enough room. You want to make sure you have a long enough tail that you can weave it in later with a darning needle. If it is too short, you will not be able to do that and your project can unravel. Better too long than too short. Second, you will pull at the end of the yarn that you're working with. The working end is what leads to the rest of your yarn. Pull it through your loop.

In step three, you'll have a slipknot created, and in Step Four you'll slip your hook through the loop, pulling on both ends of the yarn. This will tighten it. Don't tighten it to the point that it doesn't move freely down your hook. If it's that tight, then it's too tight. You want a loop that is slightly larger than your hook for ease in sliding. It should not be bigger than the thumb area of your hook.

## Slipknot

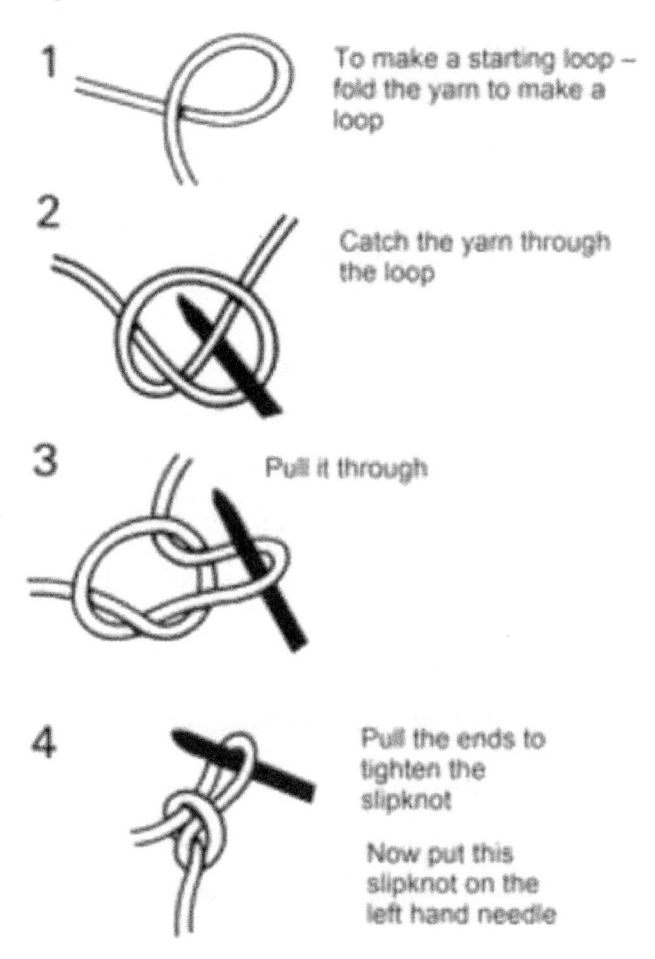

1. To make a starting loop – fold the yarn to make a loop

2. Catch the yarn through the loop

3. Pull it through

4. Pull the ends to tighten the slipknot

Now put this slipknot on the left hand needle

## Slip Ring

Making a slip ring is just like making a slip knot, but it is for a crochet round rather than a row. You start by draping the yarn over your pointer finger. The tail of the yarn should be closest to you. Then, you will twirl the other end of the yarn over the same finger and make a criss-cross. With the ball yarn over your finger, push the crochet hook through the two strands of yarn at their intersection and rotate the hook clockwise over the yarn you are working with.

Next, pull a loop down and under the ring into the center. Do a single chain stitch now, and carefully slide the loop off your finger without closing it. Work your stitches into this ring by crossing over both of the strands of yarn. Close the tail end by pulling it tight and completing the circle before continuing the round as the pattern instructs.

As you can see, the slip ring is very similar to the slip knot, just a bit larger. Therefore, once you have your slip knots down, this technique should not be hard at all to accomplish!

## Joining New Yarn Together and Switching Colors

Joining new yarn together is an important technique to master if you want to do multi-colored projects. Joining new yarn together occurs when you either run out of yarn or have to add more or when you would like to change yarn colors.

Without further ado, let's go over how to join yarn colors, or new yarn in general, together! First, take the new yarn and pull a loop of this yarn through a stitch of the last row of the yarn you are joining the new yarn to.

Use the loop as a starting point for a single crochet stitch made from the new yarn. Work in a few more stitches to make sure it is secure, then sew the end of this to the project to keep it in place.

If you are working with a square shape, it is a good idea to start the new yarn in the corner of the project to make it flow seamlessly. Start with a single crochet, then continue the line with two chains to create a double to incorporate the new yarn well.

**Fastening Off**

Fastening off your yarn is very important, for it is how you will finish your piece. It is normally the final step to a pattern, and it is how you complete your project to keep it from loosening or unraveling. To do this, you must cut your yarn from the yarn ball and leave a bit of yarn left. Take this yarn that hangs from your project and carefully sew it into your work. You will want to pull the end of it through your final stitch to secure it and draw it back up to close off the loop securely.

To sew this yarn into the end, you will need to use a tapestry needle that is large enough for your yarn. Be careful to avoid splitting your stitches and slide the needle neatly through the yarn as you complete this step.

Sew your yarn ends every time you change colors in your piece, but always fasten off your yarn at the end of its use. Do this every time you finish with a color or a pattern in general to ensure the longevity of your project.

**Adding Texture**

Adding texture to your pieces, even if it's not specified in the pattern, can add your flair and character to the project. It makes it decorative, unique, and fun! Take a plain pattern and give it life! Gather up some extra yarn and beef up your projects to wow your friends and family.

Take the crossed stitches we talked about in this chapter. For any double-crochet patterns you have, you can make panels of crossed stitches that add height and texture to the piece. You can also add ribbing with raised double crochets, which looks great on the edges of washcloths, pot holders, hats, gloves, and more.

Additionally, when a project uses single crochet stitches, you can liven it up with alternate rows of front loops or back loops! You can even add starting and ending rows of puffed stitching to add some decoration and tangible accents to mundane objects. Play around with it and see what you can come up with!

# Chapter 6. Alternative Crochet Methods

## Tunisian Crochet

Tunisian crochet is a unique form of crochet that many refer to as the afghan stitch method due to the beautiful textiles and clothing patterns that are created with this crochet style. Many use it to make decorative bags, sweaters, dresses, and more.

To perform Tunisian crochet, you will need a special Tunisian crochet hook. This is a long hook on which you build the foundation stitches off. This sets Tunisian crochet apart from traditional crochet, which does not require loop stitches over the hook at the beginning of the pattern. Now, let's go over what the Tunisian crochet stitch looks like and how it is made. First, you are going to make your foundation chain for the piece on the Tunisian hook itself. You will do this by forming the foundation chain similarly to how you would go with traditional crochet but on the hook itself. Then work your way up through each chain, picking up each loop on your way up the chain.

The next step is where you will deviate from traditional crochet. You are not going to be working the stitches back off of the hook as with normal crochet. Rather, you are going to want to make a row of stitches on the hook like you would while knitting. Once you get to the end, work a single chain without turning.

After you complete that step, hook your yarn back through the first two stitches. Then, repeat along the row after hooking the yarn again. Draw the loop through two stitches every time you do this. When you get down to a single remaining stitch, stop. At this point, you are not going to work a chain.

Instead of working a chain, start working in the opposite direction. Pass the hook through the vertical stitch and hook your yarn all the way back. Keep this new stitch on your Tunisian hook. Make another row of stitches on your hook, continuing down the row. Make sure you keep the same number of stitches on each row.

Do not add or subtract stitches, for this will mess up the overall project. It takes a bit of practice, but you can overcome it after a few tries if you concentrate. If you complete each row with the same number of stitches, just keep going in the same pattern, and you will be mastering Tunisian crochet like a pro!

## Broomstick' Crochet

Using the broomstick lace method of broomstick crochet is a unique and rather large-scale version of crochet. It is much quicker than traditional crochet, but it can be twice as satisfying due to the ease at which you can pull it off. It derives its name from the fact that broomstick crochet was first done on the large handle of a broomstick. You can use any large stick-like object to perform this craft if you'd like, or you can use your normal crochet hook along with a large knitting needle or stick to get the job done. The bigger the needle or hook you use, the larger the loops will be and thus the holes in your project. The hole-aesthetic is what you will be going for with this form of crochet, and it is quite satisfying.

To start this type of crochet, you make a foundation chain on the crochet hook. Then, you take the stick you are using and hold it firmly between your knees. Hook the yarn through every chain on the line and slip the loop onto the stick. After working the entire foundation chain and looping every stitch onto the stick, you can continue working off them.

Take your crochet hook and hook the yarn through five stitches at once while using a single crochet stitch. Then, slide the secured group of five stitches off the stick and crochet four single crochet stitches into space in the center of those loops. After you slide these stitches off, follow the rest of the row in this manner. Elongate the final single crochet stitch and slip it over the stick you are using.

Once you have done that, hook the yarn back through the top of each single crochet stitch onto the stick. You are now able to start on the next row. Work the second row precisely the same way you worked the first row, making sure not to turn the work. The following rows are the same as well.

## Crocheting with Pretty Beads

Crocheting does not have to be all about the stitches and loops! Step up your crocheting game with some pretty beads to add a bit of texture and color to your finished project. Crocheting with beads gives your projects a decorative flair and adds texture that really makes the product pop and gains some personality. You can use any colored beads that you want, and you can create a rainbow of decorative possibilities with this method of crocheting. It can be a bit tricky until you get the basics of crocheting down, but once you do, it is quite easy to learn!

The only boundaries you have to deal with is in regard to the sizes of the yarn and beads that you choose. When you get the notion to decorate your crochet projects with beads, make sure the beads are large enough for the yarn to fit through, and if you already have beads, you may need to purchase yarn that fits it. Either way, make sure your beads and yarn match up so you don't run into any problems.

There are a couple of different methods of crocheting with beads. The first method has to do with thicker yarn. If your yarn is particularly fuzzy or bulky, and your beads have holes that are on the smaller side, cut some sewing thread and double it. Then, loop the thread through a special beading needle by pulling the loop until it is more extended than the two freed ends of the thread. After this, you can thread the yarn through the loop of sewing thread and fold it back. Pick up your desired beads with the needle and then slide them through the four threads, onto the loop, and then into the loop of yarn. Repeat this with every bead you would like to get onto the yarn, making sure to keep at least one bead on the loop of yarn to keep it all together. Slide each bead down the yarn's length before adding more beads, and you will soon be able to get all of your beads onto the yarn. Once you have all the beads you want, simply snip the yarn off and remove the needle before proceeding with your crochet.

The second method is a bit simpler. If your tapestry needle is large enough, thread it with your preferred yarn. Then, slip the beads right onto the yarn!

Do the same with finer yarns and beads with smaller holes. Just use a smaller needle for smaller beads and thinner yarns.

Once your beads are securely on your yarn, simply crochet as normal for a lovely, textured pattern full of delightfully colorful beads! This creative and simple addition to your crocheting methods can really set your projects apart and make them special!

# Chapter 7. How to Understand Patterns

## What Is a Crochet Pattern?

A crochet pattern is a set of instructions, a picture, a grid, or any type of guide that shows you how to create a certain crochet project. It gives a detailed description of everything you will need to know to accomplish the desired project, and it is normally written as an abbreviated list.

## How to Read a Crochet Pattern

Before we learn how to read a crochet pattern, let's go over some of the common abbreviations that patterns use as a shorthand. They can seem like haphazard gibberish at times, so it is important to memorize the abbreviations and terms, or keep this book handy when you begin reading patterns, so you understand what they say. I will write out the full word or phrase that the abbreviation represents so you can read patterns with ease. The reason that many patterns are abbreviated is due to the fact that crocheting takes time and the patterns that layout your project can get very long and arduous very quickly if you don't shorten it down. A bit of confusion can occur when you turn to shorthand instructions, but after reading this chapter, it will be a walk in the park. The shortness of patterns through the use of abbreviations will save you time so you can focus on what you love.

Another reason that many publishers, instruction manuals, and the like abbreviate their patterns is due to cost. In the old days, when they published patterns in magazines, newspapers, and books, the cost of printing was largely determined by an amount per word or character. The longer a pattern is, the more someone who publishes it would need to pay. Therefore, shorthand was a way to make more money and retain the same information for readers. This is similar today, though, with the expanse of the internet and electronic reading, it is not as much of an issue. However, the abbreviations have stuck.

All of the patterns in this book will use full words and phrases, as this book is for beginners and abbreviations can get very confusing, but most other patterns in books or on the internet will use the abbreviations I will show you. Therefore, it's good to know them. I am sure you will want to expand your horizons and find patterns that are not in this book, and most patterns out there use these particular shorthand abbreviations across the board.

## Pattern Abbreviations

Here are all, or most, of the abbreviations that you will come across when you begin searching for crochet patterns:

- Alt – alternate
- Approx. - approximately
- Beg – beginning or beginner
- Bet – between
- Bk lp or BL – back loop
- Bl - block
- Blo – back loop only
- Bp – back post

- Bpdc – back post double crochet
- Bpsc – back post single crochet
- Bsc – beaded single crochet
- Ca – color A
- Cb – color B
- Cc – contrasting color
- Ch – chain or chain stitch
- Ch-sp – chain-space
- Cl – cluster
- Cm – centimeters
- Cont – continue
- Dc – double crochet
- Dc2tog – double crochet two together
- Dec – decrease
- Dir – directions
- Dtr – double triple crochet stitch
- Ea – each
- Est – established
- Fl or ft lp – front loop
- Flo – front loop only
- Foll – follow or follows
- Fp – front post
- Fpdc – front post double crochet

- Fpsc – front post single crochet
- Gm – grams
- Gp – group
- Gps – groups
- Hdc – half-double crochet
- Hdc2tog – half double crochet two together
- Hk – hook
- Inc – increase
- Incl – inclusive
- In – inches
- Ins – instructions
- Join – join to the first stitch of the row, normally
- Lh – left hand
- Lp – loop
- M – motif
- Mc – main color
- Mtpl – multiple
- Mtpls – multiples
- Oz – ounce
- P – purl stitch or picot
- Pat – pattern
- Pat st or patt – pattern stitch
- Pc – popcorn stitch or picot

- Pm – place marker
- Pop – popcorn stitch
- Prev – previous
- Ps – puff stitch
- Rem – remain or remaining
- Rep or rpt – repeat
- Rib – ribbing or to make the ribbing
- Rnds – rounds
- Rs – right side
- Rsc – reverse single crochet
- Sc – single crochet
- Sc2tog – single crochet two together
- Sk – skip
- Sl st – slip stitch
- Sl lp – slip loop
- Sp – space
- Sps – spaces
- Spsc – spike single crochet
- St – stitch
- Sts – stitches
- Tbl – through the back loop
- Tfl – through the front loop
- Tc – triple crochet

- Tog – together
- Turn – turn your work over
- Ws – wrong side
- Yo – yarn over(the hook)

## How to Decipher the Puzzle That Is a Crochet Pattern

Now that we have all of the abbreviations down, let's dive right into how we read a crochet pattern. Many people groan and slump over with confusion when they first see a pattern but never fear! We will decipher it here. It's really not that difficult once you get the hang of it, and once you read through these tips and explanations, you will see how easy it can be!

The first thing you should do is either keep the aforementioned list of abbreviations on hand or memorize them, for the main source of confusion regarding a pattern is the use of abbreviations. If you know those abbreviations, you are halfway to understanding the full pattern! While reading your pattern, try to say the abbreviations out loud as their full terms to clarify what the pattern is trying to say. This will help you easily glide through the pattern and get a good idea of what you will be doing.

Another good practice is to read through the pattern more than once before you even begin to attempt your project. It is easy to get lost if you start your project blind and go step by step. If the pattern is familiar in your mind, following along as your work will be much less confusing and complicated.

When there is an asterisk in your pattern, often referred to as a repeat, this is simply a way for the writer of the pattern to avoid copying the same instructions over and over again. When you get to the asterisk, it basically means that you will start back at the beginning of that row's instructions and then repeat it until the pattern says otherwise. Knowing this is a great step toward settling the confusion of a pattern, for you will see asterisks quite a lot. Keep this in mind when you read your patterns out loud, and repeat the lines with the asterisk to train your brain into recognizing the repetition involved in the project. You will not see asterisks in the patterns of this book, as it is for beginners, and I want to make it as easy to read as possible. However, you can practice reading the patterns in this book out loud to get the hang of it before turning to more challenging patterns.

Another great starting practice for reading patterns is to have someone else who is knowledgeable about crochet to read the pattern aloud to you. Hearing a pattern read to you will make it easier for you to understand it once you read it yourself. If you are new to pattern reading as well, it can be hard for your eyes to focus on the words through your confusion. Listening to the pattern helps with this.

When someone reads you a pattern, it takes out the possibility that you will lose your place in the pattern, and you can even write down an easier rendition of the pattern for yourself as you listen. Working through these issues familiarizes you with the pattern and can expand your crocheting horizons of understanding tremendously.

Additionally, until you get used to reading patterns, learn with index cards. To do this, take a stack of index cards and secure them together with yarn or some other form of thread. Then, write the title of the pattern on the top card of the stack. For every index card, write the instructions for one row on it. Make an index card for every row. This will give you a tactile visualization of the pattern, organized by row, that will be incredibly easy for you to follow. You can even write the pattern out in longhand to take out the need for abbreviations. This can be a great tool to practice pattern reading, and it will slowly train your mind to be able to read full patterns over time.

Unfortunately, it is all too common for publishers to put errors in patterns. This is something everyone will encounter at some point in regard to a pattern. When this occurs, it makes it nearly impossible to finish a pattern unless you improvise, or as I like to call it, wing it. This is where you will need to bring your crochet knowledge and practice into play. Try to figure out what the writer was trying to say, then crochet based on that. If that doesn't work, you can always try again. Crochet, in the beginning, includes a lot of trial and error. When in doubt, you can always look up similar patterns to compare results and fill in the gaps. As a bonus, if the pattern includes a picture, try to determine what types of stitches and rows were made in the picture to get a better idea of the project. You can look up pictures of similar patterns online for more clarity. Either way, it will take a bit of extra work, but you will be happy in the end when you have a beautiful finished product!

Now that we've gone over some pointers and common problems, let's break down the parts of a pattern. Every pattern should include five basic parts. These parts include the overall gauge of the piece, the size of the finished project, a list and description of needed materials, a hook size recommendation, and the main set of abbreviated instructions. The last part of that list is the bulk of the pattern, and it is what you will be working from to make the piece.

With that in mind, I am going to break down the pattern further to make it easier to understand. This way, when you read the pattern, it will make much more sense and move along at a smoother pace for you. First of all, let's go over the main part of the pattern, which are the abbreviations I listed earlier in this chapter. All, or nearly all, patterns are made up of a series of abbreviations. Abbreviations are primarily standardized across the board, so the same 'ch' you see in one pattern that means 'chain' will mean the same thing in any other pattern you read. If an abbreviation is not a standardized one, the pattern will most likely list it somewhere in the description, so you know what to do.

Next are pattern repeats. I went over this briefly when I discussed asterisks, but they can also be symbolized by brackets. The asterisk marks the start of a section that is to be repeated. Brackets encompass a whole section that needs to be repeated. They are similar, but the difference between the two needs to be noted to minimize confusion.

The parenthesis is another symbol you may see in a pattern. Parenthesis represents when a string of stitches needs to be created in the same general area. Parenthesis can also be inserted into a pattern to give you additional instructions that may not be apparent otherwise. For instance, parenthesis can tell you whether you need to be working on the right side of a piece or when you need to count certain stitches in a particular way. Stitch counts are also commonly incorporated into parenthesis to tell you the number of stitches required by the end of a row. This is often used to determine the size of your piece, and if there are numerous sizing options, it can give you an idea of the number of stitches needed for either of the sizes in a row.

The final part of a pattern that you need to take into account to know how to read the pattern in its entirety is the concept of chain multiples. At the beginning of your row in the pattern, there will be a number plus 'ch' that will indicate the number of chains you will need to create before you start row one. For instance, if a pattern says, "ch 5," you need to create four chains before starting your row.

## Pattern Charts

In addition to patterns, sometimes you will see pattern charts. The pattern chart is a visualization of the pattern that will help you understand the steps that are written in the pattern. Decoding a chart can be a bit trickier than reading a pattern, but once you know how to read the chart, it can be a really beneficial tool for keeping your project on track. Oftentimes, a chart will show a grid that represents the project you are creating. Certain symbols, such as slashes, crosses, and loops, will indicate the types of stitches that you will need to create to make your project complete. There are different types of charts, which I will go over in a moment, and they all contribute to the overall picture of your crochet piece.

There are three types of charts, which include a symbol chart, a color block chart, and a filet chart. There are also schematics or outlined drawings. A symbol chart is the type of chart that shows slashes, loops, numbers, crosses, and lines to show you the rows of the pattern you are working on. This type of chart gives the best visual of the piece as a whole, and you can easily follow along with the chart as you work in order to keep on track. Each of the symbols in this chart denotes a type of stitch or a specific instruction that is indicated in the pattern. Many crochet beginners and experts alike prefer to make projects off of a chart instead of a written pattern due to the clarity that symbol charts provide. Others like to read patterns, but it is definitely a good idea for beginners to try out symbol charts to see if it gives them a better view of their first few projects.

With a symbol chart, there will always be numbers in front of each row that tells you what row you are working on. The numbers on the right side of the chart are for stitches on the right side of the piece, and numbers that are on the left side of the chart are for stitches on the wrong side of the piece. You start the row where the number is and read it left to right for left-side numbers, and you read it right to the left for right-side numbers. They also have a symbol for each stitch on the row, so you can easily count how many stitches you will need. As for the symbols, loops normally denote a chain, and crosses, lines, and slashes represent different chain types. For instance, a cross symbol represents a single crochet stitch.

Color block charts are used for tapestries and patterns that include intarsia. They normally work from a grid with color-coded charts, and they do not often get created from written instructions. For every stitch, there is a color-coded square, and you work from the bottom up. Every color block chart comes with a key that tells you what yarns go with each color on the chart. The number of blocks in the grid will tell you the number of stitches you will need in each row. These charts are a grid-like, colorful representation of the exact piece you will be making. For instance, if you are creating a tapestry that is square and has four equal corners of color, the chart will be in the shape of a square that is split into four parts. Each part will have a color that is identical to the yarn color needed for the project, and there will be a number of squares that represent the number of stitches in the tapestry.

Filet charts are specifically for filet crochet. Filet is a crochet type that is unique in that it comes without a written pattern. These charts replace a pattern for filet, and they resemble the charts used in cross-stitch. They use tiny circles and squares that show you where you should make your stitches for the filet. For instance, there can be a large, square filet chart. It is made up of an equal number of rows made up of squares. Those squares are either blank spaces or circles, which indicate gaps in the filet or stitch blocks in the filet.

In front of each row of squares is a number that tells you what row you are on. Numbers on the right, or the odd numbers, are to be read from right to left. Numbers on the left, or even numbers, are to be read from left to right. The filled square, or the square that has a circle, indicates the block of stitches that will be crocheted into your filet piece, and open squares indicate a space between the stitched blocks. The spaces are created when you create two double crochet stitches that you separate with a pair of chains.

Lastly, schematics are used to show where you should measure important dimensions of your piece. They are drawn as an outline to give you a basic visual of the piece and its measurements. Schematics are used primarily for creating pieces of clothing, and they help you ensure that your piece is sized, so it fits perfectly with the person you are making it for. This is a modern practice that helps people create clothing for themselves, family members, friends, and for commercial use. They are often added to patterns to give people a sizing mechanism in order to make clothing easier to manipulate into a particular clothing size. It also shows you where to put items such as sleeves, collars, waistlines, and more.

Now that you know the basics of a pattern, and how to decipher it for easier reading, go take the crochet world by storm and read patterns to your heart's content! I know you can do it if you put in the practice and dedication. I promise it is not as complicated as people make it out to be!

# Chapter 8. Easy and Fun Projects

Now that you have made it to the end of this book, I bet you would like to start creating some amazing projects! You have come to the right place. In this chapter, I am going to give you many beginner-level patterns that you can master to build up your crocheting skill sets. Impress your friends, make gifts for family members, and treat yourself to some lovely creations of your very own. Let's get started!

## Tote Bag

Here is a lovely pattern for a nice bag you can carry your crochet supplies in! Bags are a bit more complicated than other patterns, but I have faith in you! Let's get the most challenging pattern in this chapter out of the way first so you have a good baseline to leap off of for the rest of these patterns. I know you can do it! Besides, who wouldn't want a beautiful hand-crocheted bag for their crochet supplies?

You can use two colors for this bag, but as this is a bit of a trickier pattern, we will stick with a single, solid color until you get the hang of it. You can always add in the second color halfway through if you feel confident enough to do so.

For this pattern, you will want a bulkier yarn. This will give the bag a sturdy but cozy look, and it will make it less likely to tear when it holds many items. Medium weight or bulky yarn should do the trick here. Worsted or Afghan material is normally the best, but as long as you go with a medium-weight yarn, you should do fine. Wool tends to be the most popular fiber type, but this too can be modified to your liking.

Go with a hook that is six to nine millimeters for this project because the yarn is fairly bulky. This will give you the dexterity you need to complete the stitches without too much of a problem. Make sure you have three balls of one hundred-gram yarn so you will not run out, then you can begin. You will be repeating this pattern twice. Once for the front half of the bag, and second for the back half of the bag. You will be sewing these two halves together. You will also be repeating the handle, as you will need two. You will be sewing these onto the body of the bag once you are finished as well.

To begin, chain thirty-two. Then, for the foundation row, do one single crochet stitch in the second chain from the hook and one single crochet stitch in each chain to the end. Thirty-one stitches should be the total here. Turn it over.

For row one, chain three, or do three double crochets, and then do one double crochet in every single crochet to the end of the row. Turn it back over. For the second row, chain one and do one single crochet to the end of the row. Turn it over once more.

Repeat the two rows until the work from the beginning measures roughly fourteen inches in length, ending in a second row. Fasten it off and repeat the process for the second part of the bag.

For the handles of the bag, you will want to repeat these next steps twice. Chain sixty-nine before starting your first row. Then, chain one and do one single crochet stitch in each chain to the end of the chain. Turn it over. Now, do the same and repeat it until the work from the beginning measures roughly four inches. Fasten it off.

Now that you have the pieces of your bag completed, sew the front of the bag to the back, leaving the top unstitched as an opening. Then, sew each side of the handle to their respective sides of the bag after folding the handle in half like a hot dog bun. Make sure to center everything before you sew it all together.

Now you have your bag! Toss in your extra crochet materials and smile at the work you have done! I knew you could do it. Let's keep going and discover some more easy patterns to get the yarn ball rolling!

# Beanie

Beanies are sweet gifts for the family, and they're quite a warm gift for yourself as well! Follow this simple pattern to create a warm winter hat for yourself and your friends! It only uses one color, so it is very easy to accomplish for beginning crocheters! This is a one size fits all pattern, but you can modify it as needed.

To begin, you will need a light yarn of a soft variety such as wool or a wool blend. Any yarn in the light category will do well, but wool will give it a nice, soft feel to it. Make sure it is a fifty-gram yarn ball with yardage of one hundred and thirty-six yards. Choose a color that makes you happy and that you would want to wear in the winter months! Next, you will want a crochet hook of four millimeters in diameter and a sewing needle to place a pom-pom at the top of the hat if you so prefer.

For the foundation ring of the hat, create four chains and join them with a slip stitch in order to complete the ring. Next, for round one, start with chain three and crochet nine double crochets into the ring. Then, join it with a slip stitch to the top of the beginning chain three. There will be ten stitches in total for row one.

For round two, create a double crochet in the same space on-chain three, then create two double crochet stitches in each of the stitches around the ring. Join it with a slip stitch at the top of the beginning chain three. There will be twenty stitches in total for round two.

For round three, create two double crochet stitches at the next stitch beside chain three. Then, at the start of the repeat, do one double crochet stitch in each of the next two stitches and two double crochet stitches in the next stitch. Repeat this from the start of repeat to the end, then join it with the slip stitch at the top of the beginning of chain three. This round will have thirty stitches in total.

For round four, go to chain three. Create one double crochet stitch in the next stitch, two double crochet stitches in the next stitch, and then repeat this from the repeat to the end. Then, join it with the slip stitch at the top of beginning chain three. There should be forty stitches in total for this round.

For round five, you will start at chain three once more. Create one double crochet stitch in each of the next two stitches. Create two double crochet stitches in the next stitch, then go to the start of the repeat and do one double crochet for each of the next three stitches. Then do two double crochet stitches in the next stitch and repeat this from the repeat to the end. Join it to the slip stitch at the top of the beginning of chain three. There should be fifty stitches in this round.

For round six, start at chain three. Create one double crochet stitch for each of the next three stitches. Do two double crochets in the next stitch, and then go to the start of the repeat and do one double crochet stitch for each of the next four stitches. Now do two double crochet stitches in the next stitch, repeat it from the repeat to the end, and join it with the slip stitch at the top of the beginning of chain three. This round should have sixty stitches.

For round seven, start at chain three and create one double crochet in each of the next four stitches. Do two double crochets in the next stitch, then start at repeat and do one double crochet for each of the next five stitches. Then, do two double crochet stitches in the next stitch. Repeat this from repeat to end and join with the slip stitch to the top of the beginning of chain three. This round should have seventy stitches.

For rounds, eight through seventeen, start at chain three and do one double crochet in every stitch in the round. Then, join with the slip stitch at the top of the beginning of chain three. For round number eighteen, start at chain one and create a single crochet in each stitch around before joining it with the slip stitch at the beginning of chain one. For round nineteen, start at chain one and create one single crochet stitch for each stitch around before joining it with the slip stitch to the beginning of chain one. Do the same with every round until you get to round number twenty-nine.

Once you finish round twenty-nine in the same fashion, fasten off and weave the ends. Then, if you prefer, attach the pom-pom with a needle and thread. Now you have your hat!

# Coasters

Coasters are a wonderful first project for those who would like to try out crochet. You can use one color of yarn and create a lovely, round coaster to enjoy for months to come. Coasters are not difficult to create, and you can make them in a wide variety of colors. They make great decorations and gifts, so why don't we give it a try? This pattern uses only one color and single crochet stitches only, so it is a very easy pattern to complete for beginners. For larger coasters, simply add two extra stitches to each round. For coasters, you are going to want to use a lightweight yarn. Wool works best for crocheted coasters, for it is one of the most absorbent materials you can work with. You can choose any yarn you like but go for one that is absorbent and has a lightweight. You will want to use a crochet hook with a diameter of four millimeters as well.

For round one, start with a slip knot and follow with two chain stitches. Create six single crochet stitches into the second chain after that. Slip stitch to join it to the end of the round. For round two, create two single crochet stitches for each following stitch. You should end with twice the number of stitches from round one, which should add to twelve if you are following this pattern exactly. Now, slip stitch to the first stitch to join the round together.

For round three, use two single crochet stitches for your next stitch and switch between one and two stitches for the rest of the round. There should be eighteen stitches at the end of this round. Slip stitch to the first stitch of this round before continuing.

For round four, create a single crochet stitch for the next two stitches, then switch to two single crochets for the next stitch. Repeat this all the way around the round until you get to the end of the circle, then make a slip stitch to join it to the first stitch in the round.

You can fasten the coaster at this point, but you can make it as large as you like. If you want to add more rounds, simply add one extra single crochet and two extra single crochets after that, then add gradually to make the circle larger. If you want a bit of a fancier border to your coaster, you can do slip stitches around the entirety of the last round for a neat look. Once you get your desired size, fasten it off, and you have a completed coaster!

# Cute Toothbrush Holder or Cup Cozy

This is a sweet project that you can use to give a bit of decorative flair and warmth to your bathroom or kitchen. These cozies fit comfortably around most small storage containers like a toothbrush holder, and they even fit around most drinking glasses. On cold nights, warm your hands with these cozies surrounding your favorite cup so you can sip on your drink comfortably. This is a very easy pattern to make, and you can use any color that speaks to you!

To begin, you will need one fifty-gram ball of fine yarn. The fine yarn gives the cozy and intricate and soft look, and it will not be so bulky that the cup cannot fit into the cozy. You want the cup or toothbrush holder to fit quite comfortably, so the fine yarn is the way to go. Additionally, you will want a crochet hook with three and a half millimeters in diameter. This will give you the most ease when creating stitches and working with the fine yarn.

The cup cozy will be about four inches in diameter when you are finished with your project. Throughout this pattern, you will be using a contrasting marker of yarn between the final stitch of the first round and the first stitch of the second round. It will help you see when you have completed the round, and it helps you not have to struggle with counting every single round. Move the marker up constantly, so you don't lose your place. Let's get started!

Start by using a slip ring. For the first row, do ten single crochets into the ring, slip stitch into the first chain, and pull the thread through to close the ring. Now, insert your marker and start round two. Do two single crochets into each stitch leading up to the marker. For round three, do one single crochet stitch into each stitch leading up to the marker. For round four, repeat to start and do one single crochet into the next stitch, then do two single crochet stitches into the following stitch. Repeat to start and repeat to repeat until you get to the marker.

For round five, repeat to start and do one single crochet into each of the next two stitches. Do two single crochets into the following stitch and repeat to start. Then repeat from the start to the marker. You now have the base of your cozy.

For round six and round seven, make one half-double crochet into each stitch to the marker. For round eight, repeat to start and do one half-double crochet into each of the next four stitches. Then do two more half-double crochets into the following stitch to repeat. Repeat from the repeat to the marker.

For round nine, repeat to start and do one half-double crochet stitch into each of the next seven stitches. Then, do two half-double crochets into the following stitch to repeat. Repeat from the repeat to the marker. For rounds ten through eighteen, do one half-double crochet into each stitch. For round nineteen, repeat to start and do one half-double crochet into each of the next eight stitches, then do two half-double crochets into the following stitch to repeat. Repeat from repeat to the marker. For rounds twenty and twenty-one, do one single crochet into each stitch.

For round twenty-two, repeat to start and do one single crochet into each of the next nine stitches. Then, do two single crochets into the following stitch to repeat. Then repeat from repeat to the marker. Fasten it off and flip the cozy inside out.

You're finished! Now, slip your favorite cup or toothbrush holder into your nice, new cozy!

# Fingerless Gloves

These gloves are comfortable, colorful, and fashionable! Easy to make and perfect for those colder months of the year, you can make these cute gloves for friends, family, and yourself! The only stitches you have to use for these gloves are single stitches, which makes this a great project for beginners who are just learning how to crochet simple patterns. You can use as many colors as you like, but since this is a beginner pattern, we are going to stick with two colors.

This pattern is for one glove, but use it twice to get the two gloves you will need to keep your hands toasty!

To begin, you are going to want a fifty-gram yarn ball that has lightweight. Pick two colors that go together in the cold months, such as white and blue. We are going to call the first color, which will be the primary color, color A. The second color you choose will be color B.

Wool yarn is great for this pattern, as it is warm and soft, but you can go with any wool blend or other yarn as long as it is in the lightweight range. It also needs to be about one hundred and thirty-six yards per yarn color in yardage.

Now that you have your yarn, you are going to want a crochet hook with four millimeters in diameter. You will also want a sewing needle of some kind in order to sew the glove halves together. Once you have that, you are ready to begin!

The foundation chain for the glove will be using color B. Make twenty-seven chain stitches for this foundation chain. For row one, start at the second chain from the hook and do a single crochet stitch. Continue this for each chain to the end, then turn the project over. For row two, start at chain one and create single crochet stitches in every stitch until you reach the end. Turn the project over once more.

From this row to the next twenty-three, totaling twenty-five rows, continue this process in single crochet. Every two rows, alternate your two colors of A and B. After you get to row ten, cut the yarn, and continue with color A. For rows ten to thirty-six, use color A, only and cease alternating the colors. Once you get to row thirty-seven, cut the yarn and switch to color B. Do two more rows in this color, then fasten off your ends and weave them together.

With the right sides together, fold each of the gloves in half and sew your side seams. Make sure you leave a gap for your thumb. Turn it right side out once you are through. That's it!

# Pot Holders

Potholders are lovely gifts that you can use to decorate your kitchen, and they are among the easiest projects to crochet. You can go with a solid color or stripes, but for this pattern, we will use a solid color so beginner crafters can finish the project with ease.

You are going to want a medium-weight yarn, and cotton normally works best for potholders. It reflects heat rather well, and it is durable enough to last for quite a while. Go with one hundred grams of yarn in order to make sure you have plenty for your potholders, but depending on how many you would like to create, you may not need that much yarn.

For the hook, you are going to want to go with a standard four-millimeter hook in diameter for this pattern. The potholder should be exactly square, and its size will be roughly six by six inches. Let's get started!

For your foundation, you will want to create thirty-seven chains. Then, do two half-double crochets together into the third and fourth chain from the hook. Start at the repeat and chain one, then add two half-double crochet stitches into the next two chains at the repeat. Next, repeat from the repeat to the repeat to the last chain before creating one half-double crochet stitch into the last chain. Now turn the project.

For row one, start at chain two and create two half-double crochet stitches together in the first and second chain spaces to repeat. Then go to chain one and create two half-double crochet stitches together in the same chain space at the last stitch and in the next chain space to repeat. Repeat from the repeat to the repeat to the end, chain one, then make one half-double crochet stitch into the top of the chain and turn the project.

For rows two through the end of seven, repeat row one. At the end of row seven, you will want to chain fourteen, then slip stitch into the first chain to make the hanging loop for the potholder. Fasten it off, and you are done!

## Simple, Flowy Scarf

This pattern is absolutely light and lovely, and it traps heat rather well. If you want something thin and beautiful to drape around your shoulders this fall or winter, look no further than this beautifully designed scarf. It is a bit complicated, but as long as you follow the pattern exactly, you will have a beautifully finished piece in no time! This pattern stops after forty-three repeats for the length, but you can continue the pattern for as long as you like to get the length that you desire.

For this pattern, you want to go with a thinner yarn, such as light or fine varieties. This makes the scarf breathable and flowy, so it gives it a delicate look. You can choose other varieties of yarn, but this is the least bulky and most delicate look you can get if you go with fine yarn instead. You will need a skein of one hundred grams to make the scarf in this pattern, but you will need more if you would like to make the scarf longer. It is all a matter of preference.

For your hook, you will want a hook with a diameter of four millimeters. This will give you the greatest level of ease while working with a finer yarn such as this. The scarf will end up with a length just shy of four feet and a width just above one foot.

To begin, create one hundred chains. Then, for your foundation row, skip five chains and repeat to two double crochets into chain one, two double crochets into the next chain, skip chain three, two double crochets, chain one, then two more double crochets into the next chain. Go to chain four, then skip six chains to repeat. Now, repeat from the repeat and end two double crochets to chain one, two double crochets into the next chain, skip three chains, do two double crochets, go to chain one, do two double crochets into the next chain, skip the next chain, then to one double crochet into the last chain and turn.

Now that the foundation row is complete, we will go to row one. Chain three, then repeat to word two double crochets, chain one, then make two double crochets into each of the next one-chain spaces. Chain three, then insert your hook under the six-chain space of the foundation chain and work one single crochet stitch. Then enclose the six-chain space and the four-chain space on the foundation row. Chain three to repeat, then repeat from repeat to repeat and end two double crochets. Chain one then does two double crochets into each of the last two one-chain spaces. Do one double crochet into space before turning the chain, then turn your project once more.

For rows two and three, chain three and then repeat work two double crochets. Chain one, then does two double crochets into each of the next two one-chain spaces. Chain four to repeat, then repeat from the repeat to the repeat. End with two double crochet stitches, then chain one and do two double crochets into each of the last two one-chain spaces. Do one double crochet into space before three chains and turn.

For row four, chain three, then repeat to two double crochets. Chain one and then do two double crochets into each of the next two one-chain spaces. Chain three, then insert the hook under the four-chain space two rows below and do one single crochet stitch to enclose both four-chain spaces. Chain three, then repeat from repeat to repeat. End with two double crochet stitches. Chain one and then do two more double crochets into each of the last two one-chain spaces. Do one more double crochet into space before the three chains and turn.

To create the length of the scarf, repeat rows two, three, and four forty-three times. After you have your desired length, fasten it off, and you have a beautiful, light, warm scarf!

# Washcloths

Good washcloths are hard to come by, so why not make your own? You can choose incredibly soft or absorbent material, and you can cater it to your own needs, color palettes, and more! Fit the aesthetic of your home and your bathroom by choosing a lovely color to match your linens and get clean, knowing you made something you are proud of!

To begin, you will want a super fine yarn, preferably cotton. Cotton works very well because it is washable, durable, and easy to work with. Many mainstream washcloths use cotton or some mixture of cotton, so they should feel natural to you when you use cotton yarn. Choose a color that fits the aesthetic of your home, or go wild! Any color will work. Make sure you get enough yarn to make as many washcloths as you like. Generally, if you want two washcloths, it would be best to go with two hundred-gram balls of yarn.

To begin, make fifty-one chains. Then, for the foundation row, do one single crochet stitch into the second from the hook, then one single crochet into each chain until you reach the end of the row. For rows one through thirty-two, start at chain one and then add one single crochet stitch into each single crochet stitch to the end. Then turn the project over.

If you would like to switch to a second color, you can do so here. Either way, work one single crochet stitch into each stitch and work chain one at the beginning of each row. Do this until you get to row fifty-two. After you reach the end of row fifty-two, fasten it off, and you have a lovely washcloth!

# Broomstick Crochet Scarf

Last but not least, let's end these bonus patterns with a unique pattern! It seems fitting, no pun intended, that we end the bonus patterns with a broomstick crochet technique to test out our brand-new skills! This simple pattern will wow your friends and family with its beautiful design and warm feeling! The finished product will be around sixty inches long and about five inches wide, but you can always make it longer by adding more rows or wider by adding extra stitches.

To begin this pattern, get a large stick, knitting needle, broom handle, or any large stick-like object that is bigger than your normal crochet hook. The easiest of these to work with is a knitting needle, but it is up to you!

Now, you will want to use a yarn that has a mild but beautiful color, and the easiest yarn weight to use would be either a fine or a light yarn. Make sure you have at least three fifty-gram balls of yarn for this project. Get more for a longer scarf if that is what you prefer. If you are using a knitting needle, I would suggest using one that is twenty millimeters in diameter or size thirty-five. Then, use a crochet hook that is three and a half millimeters in diameter. Lastly, you will need a tapestry needle for fastening off the finished project.

Let's get started with this delightfully rustic pattern! First, use your crochet hook and make thirty-five chains. Once this is complete, you will begin row one by placing the loop from your crochet hook onto the knitting needle or your stick of choice. For the purpose of this pattern, and to minimize confusion, I will hereby refer to it as a knitting needle, but remember that you can use whatever you prefer for this pattern. Once the loop is on the knitting needle, go to the start of the repeat and repeat from this to the repeat to the end. Make thirty-five loops in total.

For row two, start at the repeat and use the crochet hook to work a single crochet stitch through the middle of the first five loops. Work four more single crochet stitches into that same replace and repeat. Repeat from start to end. Keep your loops on the knitting needle until your first single crochet to keep your five loops secured, then sleep each group off the needle and do the next four single crochets. There should be seven groups in total.

For the third row, place your loop from the hook on the knitting needle. Skip your first single crochet, then start at the repeat. Insert your hook into the next single crochet stitch, put the yarn over the hook, then draw your loop through and slip it all onto the knitting needle. Repeat from start to end. There should be thirty-five loops.

Repeat the second and third-row until your scarf gets to your desired length, but make sure to end on row two. For this pattern, that is sixty inches, but you can make it as long as you like. Once you have your desired length, fasten it off, and you have a gorgeous scarf!

# Conclusion

Thank you for making it to the end. Crochet stitching is an art that dates back to a few centuries and is still alive today. These easy tips and tricks we learned will surely help you get a great feel of this art and you'll eventually master it. All the crochet styles are fairly easy and require a good amount of practice. Yes, the machines have taken over most of the industrial fabric stitching, but this art is as valuable today as it was in the earlier days of crochet styles.

The patterns used in this stitching will be further enhanced as time progresses since the new generation has welcomed it and has given it a new life. Crochet patterns have also taken over the new kind of projects, which are called DIY (do it yourself). You can become an expert in crochet stitching and are very likely to start a home-based online shop of handicrafts.

You can make numerous things out of stitching such as designs on the clothes or fixtures which you have to make on your dresses. If you are a woman and you are trying to get it done, then this is the best guide for you to get started, which will help you learn what things you need to keep in your bag as well as when you step out in case of emergency.

Crochet stitching allows you to keep getting your hands into something new and valuable. There are hundreds and thousands of new designs in crochet stitching from different countries around the globe, involving new and traditional designs to get a feel of it and hone your skills, ultimately helping you either in commercial or private usage. Various products can be weaved using crochets such as scarves, shawls, etc., which are eye-grabbing and in fashion at the same time.

Your home is your haven, your castle. It's the most personal space you have. It's where most of the important events in your life, and your family's life, take place. You build your relationships there. You nurture your hopes and dreams there. You raise your children there. You grow old there.

There's no better way to personalize a space that is so intimately yours than with everyday objects you make yourself. An expensive mattress covered in high-end sheets is very comfortable, but you can't wrap yourself in them and remember the weekend you spent making them with a smile on your face. A fancy couch looks great in your living room, but the cushions you crocheted bring it an added touch that marks it as yours.

It can be intimidating to think about making objects for your home. They sound big and scary. They sound like the kind of thing that should take weeks or months, the labor of love your grandmother told you about. Those projects are out there, and they can be a lot of fun to work on too. But it's okay to get your feet wet. Go ahead and treat yourself to the satisfaction of seeing a project through from beginning to end in a single weekend. You'll end up with a lovely finished product, and you'll build up the confidence to tackle those bigger projects a little further down the road. Learning to crochet is a skill that you will find useful because you can take what you learn and turn it into garments and projects that provide joy and utility for people who use them. There is a large variety of uses for the crochet stitches covered. With your imagination, you can take your new knowledge of the stitches and create your own patterns and designs to make a variety of projects of your own.

Keep your hands relaxed so that you are not tensing up and tiring your fingers and hands. By relaxing, your stitches will come freely, and by practicing, you will be able to unravel the stitches that don't measure up to your standard, retry the stitches over and over again. You will find that you like some stitches more than others. By mastering the basic stitches, you will be able to tolerate your least favorites. The first row is always the most grueling. Make sure your foundation chain is even and not too tight. This will make it easier to fit the hook into the chain when you are making the first row of stitches. It will come easier as time goes by, and you practice more.

Take the stitches you have learned and make swatches of the stitches. This practice will pay off handsomely as you perfect the stitches and grow comfortable handling crochet hooks of different sizes. Practicing is the best way to feel good about your skills. You will be able to see how much easier the stitches are made when you are familiar with how the yarn feels in your hands and how it moves along the crochet hook. It takes away the intimidating features of crochet. The language of crochet is defined, and the patterns are explained in plain English. Join the crochet community by putting your new skills into action. Make the projects and you'll see why people enjoy crochet and all that it has to offer. Relax and enjoy using what you learn to produce real items that can please you.